Psychotherapy
and the
Creative Patient

Psychotherapy and the Creative Patient

E. Mark Stern, Editor

Iona College, New Rochelle, New York

The Haworth Press
New York • London

Psychotherapy and the Creative Patient has also been published as *The Psychotherapy Patient*, Volume 4, Number 1 1987.

The Haworth Press, Inc., 12 West 32 Street, New York, NY 10001
EUROSPAN/Haworth, 3 Henrietta Street, London WC2E 8LU England

Library of Congress Cataloging-in-Publication Data

Psychotherapy and the creative patient.

    Has also been published as: The Psychotherapy patient, v. 4, no. 1 1987.
    Includes bibliographies.
    1. Psychotherapy. 2. Creative ability. I. Stern, E. Mark, 1919- . [DNLM:
1. Creativeness. 2. Psychotherapy. W1 PS87 v.4 no.1 / WM 420 P97534]
RC454.4.P84   1988   616.89'14   88-2694
ISBN 0-86656-642-2
ISBN 0-8656-831-X (pbk.)

Psychotherapy and the Creative Patient

CONTENTS

ABOUT THE EDITOR

E. Mark Stern, EdD, completed his clinical studies at Columbia University and at the Institute of the National Psychology Association for Psychoanalysis. In addition to his private practice in psychotherapy and psychoanalysis, Dr. Stern is Professor in the Graduate Division of Pastoral Counseling, Iona College, New Rochelle, New York, and he is on the faculty of the American Institute for Psychotherapy and Psychoanalysis in New York City. Dr. Stern is a Diplomate in Clinical Psychology of the American Board of Professional Psychology and Fellow of the American Psychological Association.

Psychotherapy and Creativity:
An Awakening of Archetypes—
A Preface

We should invert our eyes and practice a sublime astronomy in the infinitude of our hearts. . . . If we see the Milky Way, it is because it *actually exists in our souls*.

Leon Bloy

What erupts . . . is none other than the secret drive of all human and superhuman desire to step beyond the limits of creaturehood and at least feel free—free like the creative God.

Schulze-Maizier
From his introductions to
sermons of Meister Eckhart

The creative imperative serves as a mark of passion. From the earliest moments of the psychotherapeutic relationship, the creative alliance of patient and therapist remains the means of the process. Free association as an attempt to reach the locus or inner source acknowledges the therapeutic paradox in its claim to analyze, interpret, synthesize, and challenge. The open spirit of this engagement becomes the heartland of the psychotherapeutic endeavor.

In the improvisations enacted by the two or more parties involved in a therapeutic endeavor, hopes are raised for a creative antidote. Hope as the creative force behind free associations and other therapeutic soliloquies, dialogues, trialogues, and such is nonetheless entwined with the swell of dormant archetypes. Archetypal constituents of the soul provide the creative vantages. These band together a light and darkness—death and rebirth. The text of the individual is linked to the multifaceted vision of the archetypes. These are quartered within the person and collective imagination. While the text is

1

ultimately personal and internal, it often appears as the restless repertoire of interactions with others.

What then is the purpose of psychotherapy with creators? Creative patients are those who discern dynamic relationships. Their creativity blends the emergence of life-propelling fantasies and their accompanying terrors. It is here that even traumas lead to alterations of consciousness, eventually heading into a healing uniqueness of their own.

Emotional traumas are thus the probable stimuli for new awakenings. The woman whose auditory hallucinations serve as shadows of her passions; the frustrated student whose inner distractions may introduce newer perceptions of the external world; the disruptive adolescent whose rebellion acts as a vehicle out of the cesspools of poverty; or the depressed elder whose impasse was broken when he learned to rail against the quicksands of mediocrity. These are a sampling of creative patients.

According to Meek (1985) "the ground of creativity is freedom (but) this ground of creativity is beyond . . . confinement" (p. 195). The essence of what is creative is the legacy of newer modes of awareness and individuation. Even within compulsivity, rigidity, and obsession, a grounding is established for a struggle against confinement. The spurring on of creative forces awakens the excitement inherent in existence.

The fear of formlessness may hamper newer levels of awareness. In such cases psychotherapy can employ those wits that may help release the individual from the terrors of spontaneity. In providing both respite and insight, the therapist's endeavor encourages the enlistment of those dynamic parts which, with appropriate and skilled encouragement, can yoke into new wholes.

The creative endeavor, apart from its instrumental functions, transforms that which is fixed by moving beyond the stereotypes into archetypes. Archetypes have a decisive function in the history of culture as well as in the individual. An awareness of archetypal foundations is a creative endeavor. The creative awareness of archetypal underpinnings becomes for any one person his or her statement of becoming. The dormant energies released by such awareness demonstrate the true value of creative freedom. What ensues are sources and energies that taken on organizing functions, each confirming the individual's place in history. Each of the archetypes shapes history. Their enlistment as realities in psychotherapy helps transcend that which alienates and isolates.

James Hillman (1983) reckons with that which makes for a psychologically creative person through an appeal to the archetypal backgrounds and fantasies. It is these images that are evoked as points of re-cognizing one's fullest potentialities. They form the basis of all creative knowledge because of their involvement through the imagination of a spiritual regeneration. Psychotherapy adds meaning inasmuch as it challenges anything fixed in those archetypal impressions that move people.

Psychotherapy, in its willingness to remain watchful, evokes the creative impulses. Its efforts alone spur a unique way of being heard. In so doing the process concentrates its efforts in the expansion of a multimodal means of reversing emotional confinement. This healing relationship draws its sustenance from the uniqueness of each individual's uses of the qualitative laid bare by newer levels of care and communication.

Creativity must be reverenced if it is to remain as that experience which awakens in psychotherapy (Stern, 1966). But how? As both a celebration of individual inspiration and as the movement away from the unmovable sources. Creativity thus becomes that empowerment which enables the individual appreciate that vision of doing via undoing, or undoing fixed positions as a means of cleansing and purifying the psychotherapy initiate for healing and regeneration.

Gathered in this volume are a series of disparate but cohering ideas meant to awaken a therapeutic sensitivity. Creativity is a joint and collective process and together these essays become additions to the areas of discovery and aesthetics as much as to the theory and practice of psychotherapy. In their variations on a theme, the contributions to this volume have continued to stress a complex (though hopefully not a complicated) statement regarding an area only occasionally addressed in psychotherapeutic literature.

E. Mark Stern
Editor

REFERENCES

Hillman, J. (1983). *Interviews: Conversations with Laura Pozzo on psychotherapy, biography, love, soul, dreams, work, imagination, and the state of culture.* New York: Harper & Row.

Meek, C.R. (1985). *Existence, culture and psychotherapy.* New York: Philosophical Library.

Stern, E.M. (1966). Psychotherapy: Reverence for experience. *Journal of Existentialism,* 6(23), 279-287.

The Enlarged Repertoire:
An Exchange

E. Mark Stern
Virginia Fraser Stern

SUMMARY. A dialogue between two psychotherapists, highlighting the notion of creativity as a force in all psychotherapeutic encounters. Emphasis is placed on "approach" and "leap" in contrast to therapeutic technique. Creativity is further seen in patients as "courage," "remaining spontaneous," "transcending what others think." Psychotherapy is considered as the process of helping to awaken one's responses as a way of moving beyond the repetition of reactive transference.

Virginia Fraser Stern: Is it right to claim that treating a creative person is all that unusual? Patients who are by profession poets, artists, or writers highlight the same survival or bread-and-butter issues that most adults struggle with. These creative patients, like others, try to find meaning and purpose in work. I don't know that that's all that different from most "noncreative" people. But perhaps the term noncreative is a misnomer. I know people who are

---

E. Mark Stern, EdD, completed his clinical studies at Columbia University (1955) and at the Institute of the National Psychological Association for Psychoanalysis. Besides his private practice in psychotherapy and psychoanalysis, Dr. Stern is Professor in the Graduate Division of Pastoral Counseling, Iona College, New Rochelle, New York, and is on the faculty of the American Institute for Psychotherapy and Psychoanalysis in New York City. Dr. Stern is a Diplomate in Clinical Psychology of the American Board of Professional Psychology and Fellow of the American Psychological Association. Mailing address: 215 East 11 Street, New York, NY 10003.

Virginia Fraser Stern, MS, Columbia University School of Social Work, is presently a full-time candidate for the PhD degree in Health Psychology at Ferkhauf School of Psychology, Yeshiva University, New York City. She has a part-time private practice in psychotherapy in New York City. Mailing address: 215 E. 11 Street, New York, NY 10003.

5

very creative, but are not so defined by vocation. Their creativity is manifest in the stances they take and in their attempts to integrate thoughts, ideas, and activities.

E. Mark Stern: Are there not two issues on the drawing boards? One, whether "creative patient" as a category is viable. Two, whether we can treat people creatively.

VFS: Therapists describe themselves as creative people who help others find integration and meaning in their lives.

EMS: My day may not always be creative. I sometimes find myself uncreatively alienated. But there are those times when I feel a special (creative?) context emerging. Both occasions are important. Sometimes creativity means to stand in waiting while the patient gradually comes forth. But many of my most exciting moments take place when I am fully in touch or engaged with the patient. Patients destruct or deconstruct. It is my obligation to help them see these patterns relate to what most reflects what Carol Gratton (1980) has called "the original self," that is a "vital connection to their understanding of the underlying directedness of their lives" (p. 44).

VFS: It takes creative therapists to engage what is creative in the patient. Like the artist, such therapists are inspired. The act of creation is to be found in the therapeutic relationship. It is the patient who is finally the source of the inspiration.

EMS: Creation then is a joint project happening within the therapeutic moment. Together the therapeutic and the creative imply mutation. Each fosters a special excitement finally transformed into change. The therapeutic happens between parent and child, spouse and spouse, friend and friend, physician and patient, artist and medium. In each of these interchanges there is communion. I rarely think of specific techniques or approaches in psychotherapy, but rather of periods of darkness and light. Witnessing another with all of oneself is what counts.

VFS: Witnessing stands in stark contrast to technique. People come into therapy knowing what they need and want even though they may not be able to verbalize it. As therapist, my job is to help patients hear what it is that they already know about their own lives. This, I am convinced, is the receptivity of the creative moment.

EMS: Such moments are faith-filled leaps.

VFS: You mentioned earlier that it is not possible to be creative every minute. It is an illness of our age that anyone might think that there should be some sort of connected inspiration every second of the day. Certainly it's important not to lose hope, but hope always stands in wait and quiet expectation.

EMS: I quite agree. Those who claim to be ceaselessly creative are more properly committed to a life of performance.

VFS: Considering what makes for a creative growing and deepening relationship, it becomes clear that each party must first of all be willing to abide with the other. There are, in contrast, anxious couples who are concerned that not always being excited by the other means that the relationship is about to crumble. Truly creative couples have a profound notion of the permanency of their commitment. Knowing this permanency as essence, they are naturally aware that they can afford to bear low periods of relating. Life together may not be easy, and they may need some help struggling through the more difficult periods, but the relationship itself is not what's in question.

Creativity is an essential durability. It includes inspiration. One may not always connect, and there will be low periods. It may be hard to get to at times. But the charge is to continue the struggle.

EMS: Or not to lose hope in the struggle, even as the struggle itself is to keep faith. Nothing simple here. We're talking of the *work* of creativity, not necessarily its inspiration. The work of creativity is to follow through. Not mere performance — no flash in the pan. Living a life in which the protagonist is exclusively committed to performance is drivenness. Where there is mere drivenness, performance needs to *always* be "on."

VFS: You're talking about confusing product and quality, about the notion of running around in circles in order to be busy all day. But what about the action of truly connecting?

EMS: There are different modes of drivenness. I once knew a concert pianist who regularly toured local communities playing the same scores night after night with consistent inspiration. Another gentleman appeared to be almost confined to his one-room apartment. He felt incapable of moving into the social community, much less able to unpack his suitcases even after a year and a half. But this was appearance. Our work in therapy revealed a unique repertoire of mystical and philosophic inspirations. When he trusted enough, these inspirations came through, and not as mere recitations. Despite appearances, the creative self came forth in both cases.

VFS: I would bet they both sought you out because of their needing a place to find the courage and support to further actualize these "activities."

EMS: A significant percentage of people come into therapy looking for what amounts to a confirming relationship. Others may come with the idea of avoiding their creativity and thus distort the relationship. They come looking for specific tutorial services rendered by "an expert." It hardly matters who the expert is or what the state of his or her soul. What counts is a noncreative dependence. I recall John Rosen, a psychiatrist who over the years has worked with psychotic patients, saying that the degree of senseless transference can be so intense as to have little to do with who the therapist is. Such transference is by nature a one-sided dependence and ultimately noncreative. Creativity, in the sense that we are using it here, resides within those boundaries of a therapeutic relationship that allow for the integration of seemingly disparate elements of a patient's life. Creativity thus becomes the active ensemble of two or more people acting with the inspirations of a *particular* moment in time.

For several years I have worked with groups of frustrated writers, exceptionally talented teachers who have "lost it," underperforming musicians, and other creatively blocked patients. Blocked is not laziness. Nor is it appropriate to say that there is a definable genesis to the damming up of a created project. Creation needs blockage as much as it needs construction. Texts are often subverted, that is, moved into *sub* versions. These hidden texts provide a lesser known aspect of inspiration. Often a "block" is required in order that gratification may have its myriad expressions. Herbert Marcus (1962) wrote of a logic of gratification standing against a backdrop of repression. The sensuousness of creation literally requires a new mode of being alive in order for it to be awakened. In practical terms, regression helps the potential creator move away from self-consciousness. If the sub-version of creation is to be reborn, humility and, yes, blocks are required before the actualized artistic version can come to be.

VFS: Some artists who have difficulty with their own work are frequently victims of workaholism or overproductivity. They become so involved in what they're producing that they lose touch. This loss often insures they remain out of touch with their souls. Becoming comfortable with the idea of their many lost facets involves a suspension of expectations of being a certain kind of person or artist.

EMS: People who have performance orientations (i.e., workaholism) overshadow their deeper itineraries. Resisting such tendencies has its value. People who have felt much fear of not "coming through" are like those with a history of early abuse. Their own inner resources are linked to what must come through—or else!

VFS: There is of course a danger in looking to these early sources. If you work with a patient long enough, what happened in childhood becomes paramount. All the more reason to ask, "Are you going to keep blaming your mother, father, teacher, older siblings, or early life situation for your obsession with performance? Or are you somehow taking responsibility for who you are and not what you make today?"

* * *

VFS: Creativity is in constant relationship with the muse of inspiration. Once a project is finished—a thought, an act, or whatever—it's in the beyond. The creator is on to the next thing. What I am aware of is the process—not to be confused with a manic hyped-up overreaction.

EMS: For purposes of our discussion I'd like to highlight those psychotherapy patients who appear to live for their therapy and seem to have very little else to do. One woman, a sculptor, has had to endure so much strife in her artists' cooperative that therapy seems to be all she can manage. She finds that her sessions are like practicing scales. They are absolutely essential to where she is at the moment. It's now been eight months since she has produced a piece of sculpture. This stands in contrast to a performance orientation. She rightly fears that performing at this point would be "showing *them*" and little else. Sort of living in other people's eyes and forsaking her own vision.

VFS: There is a certain wonderment in the actions of a very young child. Movement, change, stimulation, and unself-conscious searching and sound characterizes the debut in the social milieu. Then suddenly there comes a developmental surge in which the child is still busy, but now suddenly wonders, "Who's watching me?" "Do they think I'm cute?" "Are they dazzled with what I'm doing?" "Something has changed!" A creative nub appears to have shifted. This then becomes a temptation to give way to or to be courageously resisted. As the person grows older the fruitful task is to gain the courage of learning to become receptive to the inner voice of inspiration while consciously shutting out the stares or judgments of others.

EMS: Courage may well be a synonym for creativity. It is that willingness to take responsibility for reflection. "Reflection," as noted by Gabriel Marcel (1960) "is never exercised on things . . . (but is) a personal act . . . which nobody else would have been able to undertake in my place, or on my behalf" (p. 97). This is awareness, but awareness as creativity.

VFS: When the young child first becomes aware of his or her doings and how these doings are being perceived by others, the real task is to remain spontaneous. As one moves through the life cycle, it remains crucial to keep in touch with the sort of courage to remain free of concerns of how "they see me."

EMS: But one does need to know one is linked to the world. So isn't it vital to know how one is being seen? To really understand that is to be self-affirming.

VFS: True. Creativity in adulthood calls for a sense of being in and within the world. Certainly an artist wants to be able to show his or her paintings. But that means learning to hear criticism and perhaps scorn as well as acceptance and gratitude. Mainly the person has to be able to tune out the stares of others when accomplishing the necessary work.

EMS: I agree, I think of a necessary transcendence or rising beyond what others think. Yet in another gear—the shift to psychotherapy—isn't it true that it's the patient's orientation to want to please? For some, *not* to please is to perish. For others, the act of pleasing involves a feeling of inward satisfaction.

Working creatively with a potentially creative patient means encouraging another to move into his or her own creative act. The temptation to bring that person beyond his or her felt need is probably banal. Psychotherapy is meant to help awaken a patient to respond, rather than merely react to the world. Art is that common denominator that, as a therapeutic endeavor, awakens that extra degree of grace or sensibility so that the person may develop into a most personal sense of the extraordinary. A life needs such moments.

VFS: Although no person can ultimately pay attention to what others want during moments of creation, they do often want some guidance or in some cases permission in order to confront dormant abilities as well as those necessary skills that are geared to tune out the temptation to merely cater to what the "world" compulsively appears to want. Confronting self in this sense reaches into inner creative resources. A warning is probably appropriate. Those busily confronting such talents may well find themselves at odds with their outdated and often unsuccessful survival tactics.

EMS: But perhaps some who are so concerned with others might actually be in better tune with what others need of them. It's always a very fine line. After all, to totally disregard is experienced as being disregarded. A therapist must make the best use of this dilemma.

Often to regard a patient as "creative" and "beyond the world" may bring about an unholy alliance. It is in such instances that the therapist can become something of an encumbrance, can even become autocratic. Yet there is another side. If the therapist is in communion with the patient's perspective then the spiritual aspects of a mutual creativity will take effect.

VFS: Autocracy breeds rescue fantasies, but little in the way of relationship. The hard work needed in doing therapy is that priceless art of learning to step aside. Only by stepping aside can one provide the necessary atmosphere inherent in creativity. It is potential that is always in process, the process of continual expansiveness. The relationship becomes the muse that inspires.

EMS: Yes, a lot of work is involved in standing with and aside an other. Is it also true that some patients are willing to stick with therapy as a work in process?

VFS: Work within the therapeutic relationship breeds those special moments that make for the work of real communication. Such moments may indeed be quite rare. Perhaps only a fraction of the time spent in therapy is actually work. But the rest of the solidifying process in therapy hinges on such creative moments.

EMS: I'd like to say that these moments happen when there is a gathering of the many disparate elements into a meaningful whole.

VFS: I have patients who maintain a distinctive achievement orientation. With them, there is this tendency to rate each of the sessions. Comments like "Did I get anywhere last session?" or "Boy! I really moved ahead today—so many insights!" It's been my observation that therapy really begins to work when they stop saying such things. Quantification can be antitherapeutic.

EMS: I recall part of a poem by an Eastern mystical teacher (Chogyam Trungpa, 1972:47) that says much to me about the therapeutic process.

> Sometimes it is tedious,
> Tedious because you're hopeful
> Hopeful for something to happen.
> Sometimes it is creative
> And your heart is open
> To creativity.
> These two manifestations
> Are clearly seen
> Alternatively,
> Pain and pleasure alike.
> It is what is.

You can't in fact do the work of psychotherapy without appreciating these alternating modes of the same product. What is required is a posture, a finesse, which can best deal with these alternating phases. To merely try for efficiency, for a product, loses a sense of the fuller engagement.

VFS: Like the computer program whose 1000 random phrases do give content but never context.

EMS: I've seen sophisticated biofeedback instrumentation that eerily instills a sense of trust and ease, but trust in what? Engagement in what? There is a temptation to build a *golem* — a relationship without an engagement.

* * *

VFS: Who is my creative patient is misleading. Better said, are they the poets, the writers, the actors, the painters? There are those days when I don't think any of them are creative, and when I don't think I'm very creative either. Yet in thinking about therapy and about how one approaches it, I'm convinced that every one of my patients is creative. On another note, what of the danger of the practitioner who is self-labeled as a therapist for creative people?

EMS: Ultimately there are no specialties in the field of psychotherapy. Even so, I'm willing to see creative encounters as occasional. Creativity, when it arises, serves as the hub of potential change. Some will never meet these criteria. Many will insist on the prescription mode. Yet even here, engagement may happen. When, why, how, is best acknowledged as a legitimate array of questions. Yet there are no appropriate answers to these questions.

VFS: The poem you cited earlier spoke of tedium — humdrum moments — alternating with creativity. I am often surprised by patients whom I have found lagging in interest, often wondering where is this therapy going. How often I've been pulled up by my bootstraps by suddenly seeing a great moment. I do have to remain humble to what may be happening.

EMS: My sense is that there is a creative challenge within each therapeutic relationship. I worked with a man whom one might call quite resistive to therapy. He spoke freely about business and surface plans for a new mortgage. There was little sense of his feelings. Our eyes seem to avoid each other most of the time. The struggle for that gaze ultimately became the creative motif in our work. I did learn that, as a youngster, he dared not look at the richer kids in his neighborhood. His father was a superintendent of a large luxury apartment house where they lived in a basement flat. The very aversion I experienced created an atmosphere that moved far beyond what might be termed a transferential stand-off. One day our eyes made a moment of contact. That moment, sometimes duplicated, finally melted into what I termed a redeeming otherness.

VFS: Such aspects of contact live on preverbal levels. It's often there that people know what and who they want. It's not for me to write prescriptions for people since they know what they need better than I do. Occasionally someone who is in therapy for an extended period of time may well question what he or she is still trying to work out. If it's been a quite repetitious process with little sense of newness, I might even begin to question my own integrity in continuing to see such a person. But, given the creative moment, I might begin to note that that person is by and large dedicated to the process of therapy.

You have to be aware that patients eventually get around to acknowledging when the resistance has progressed so that it provides enough security to allow for gazes to meet. It certainly can take a long time for these developments to happen. When it does, it blazons within a trusting engagement.

EMS: The shadow is also interesting. I have been very humbled over the years by those occasions in which patients reject me after one or two consultations. I feel it important to keep faith that these persons intuitively exercise a creativity of their own. It was that I was not the person who could best keep track of their pace or follow the subtleties of their lingo.

VFS: Therapists need to know that the most qualitative of their art doesn't always work. From my own experience, I know that when my children were little, it was easy to think that I could take care of all their needs. But when they got to be adolescents they were able to locate other adults who honed in on their needs and in some cases better than I did. Roles have to be constantly renegotiated when raising children and when doing therapy. Both are creative endeavors in learning how to let go.

EMS: When an artist has a retrospective exhibition, hints of the many detours and "mistakes" are seen. Artists are artists because of their ability to transcend contradictions while incorporating them into creations.

VFS: Wonderful as the creations or products are, they are not the process. The therapeutic situation is always the process.

EMS: Process indicates the broad repertoire of creative challenges. Only through a patient process can therapy move beyond the transference. Allowing for the emergence of many roles allows for the larger repertoire. The patient's creativity rests with his or her seeing the therapist and others in a context that draws the best that can be received and contributed to. In a Utopian sense, the patient will then, and then only, be less interested in extinguishing psychopathy than in extending the possibilities in life.

REFERENCES

Chogyam Trungpa. (1972). *Mudra*. Berkeley, CA: Shambala.

Gratton, C. (1980). Approaching a formative context for direction of the original self. *Studies in Formative Spirituality*, 1(1), 41-53.

Marcel, G. (1966). *The mystery of being: Reflection and mystery* (G.S. Fraser, Trans.). Chicago: Gateway.

Marcuse, H. (1962). *Eros and civilization: A philosophical inquiry into Freud*. New York: Vintage.

The Creative Patient:
A Variety of Therapy Models
and Techniques

Robert J. Dunn

SUMMARY. This article examines issues related to conducting effective psychotherapy with creative patients. Contemporary psychological viewpoints regarding human creativity are surveyed. As well, the relationships among creativity, intelligence, and personality are explored.

Three common patterns representative of creative individuals in psychotherapy are described via the research literature and clinical vignettes. These three patterns are: (1) the creating individual at odds with his/her environment, (2) thwarted creativity, and (3) creativity with severe psychopathology.

The article suggests that a variety of therapy models and techniques have shown some effectiveness with creative patients. While not unimportant, these therapy variables may be less significant than therapist variables (e.g., style, personal attributes) in effecting positive therapy outcome with the creative.

Psychotherapy might be viewed as a process in which the therapist and the creative patient fashion an understandable "self-metaphor," representative of the patient's dysfunctional status. Effective therapy, via techniques and process, reconstructs this dysfunctional self-metaphor or, in some cases, may construct an alternative, more adaptive self-metaphor. Clinical examples of this metaphor construction process are given.

In creativity, the ability to register or differentiate similarities from manifold experience is the common guiding principle – a

---

Robert J. Dunn received his PhD in clinical psychology from Iowa State University in 1974. For nine years he was Head of Psychology at St. Boniface General Hospital in Winnipeg, and Associate Professor of Psychiatry at the University of Manitoba, Canada. He is currently Associate Professor of Psychology and Clinical Director of the Student Counseling at Loras College. Mailing address: Department of Psychology, Loras College, Dubuque, IA 52001.

tremulous little light with which to search and attain, with which to break the secret of the universal night and make a piece of understanding a piece of ourselves. (Arieti, 1967, p. 453)

CREATIVITY

Models of Creativity

The very nature of the creative process seems private, metaphoric, abstract, and inferential, at odds with the tools of science. It is indeed a tribute to science's creativity that, despite a myriad of difficulties, it has persevered in examining the structures and processes of human creativity. While we have, at best, an incomplete understanding of creativity, our knowledge of it is growing and deepening.

Galton's (1869) research with eminent men generally marks the beginning of the modern era of studying exceptional human qualities. Interest focused on studying and measuring individual differences in psychological traits and invoking hereditary-based explanations for psychological differences. This use of empirical methods and applied statistics developed into the psychometric or trait tradition. Over succeeding decades, psychometric and trait approaches have concentrated on the quantitative measurement of intelligence and on behavioral and cognitive concomitant of high IQ (Barron, 1969; Cox, 1926; Pressy, 1949; Terman, 1925; Torrance, 1971).

While primarily interested in the study of genius, contemporary proponents of the trait approach have stopped equating genius and creativity. The latter term has come to denote high intelligence *plus* certain personality features such as self-sufficiency, dominance, stability, and readiness to persevere and face difficulties (Cattell & Butcher, 1968). The notion that a certain average or above-average intelligence is a necessary but not sufficient condition for creativity seems to sum up the current perspective on this relationship (Albert, 1980). Intelligence and creativity are thus seen as multifaceted, partially overlapping human attributes (Anastasi & Schaefer, 1971; Guilford, 1971). A modern factor-analytic model (Schmukler, 1982) cites three core factors underlying creativity — original and high quality information processing, expressive imagination, and social competence.

Cognitive psychology, as expected, has emphasized the intellectual, information-processing components of creativity, relating it to original and particular styles of thinking and problem solving. The creative person is described as divergent thinking and cognitive complexity (Alpaugh & Birren, 1977). Jacques (1964) notes age-related styles of creativity, with young adults evidencing an intense, spontaneous, "hot from the fire" creativity, and middle-age and older adults demonstrating more of a "sculpted" creativity, thoughtful and worked through. Kagan (1984), in studying creative children, finds that they search for the unusual, take delight in generating novel ideas, and are not apprehensive about making mistakes. Creative problem solving is described as daring, intuitive, motivated by intrinsic, theoretical and aesthetic values. Dacey (1982) outlines two theories as to how the mind of a creative person works: (1) *associationism*, by which parts of a problem are synthesized in new innovative ways and (2) *structuralism*, in which whole problems are restructured. Getzels and Csikszentmihalyi (1975) suggest creativity may be more in the ability to *find* and *define* problems, that is, finding the right problem to solve. Highly creative individuals are characterized by mental risk taking and the ability to flexibly process large quantities of information.

Guilford (1984) provides a hybrid approach, utilizing both psychometric and cognitive traditions with his structures of intellect model. He cites divergent production as the key process in creative thinking. The creative person is seen as fluent, flexible, original, sensitive, elaborative, and able to redefine.

Almost from its inception, psychoanalysis has contributed to our understanding of creativity, often using case studies and psychohistories to examine the roots of individual creativity. Freud (1913) emphasizes intrapsychic dynamics and interpersonal conflict in its understanding. The classic psychoanalytic approach concerns itself primarily with artistic creativity, associating it with pathological states, neuroses, unconscious motives and symbolism (Ihanus, 1982).

Neo-analytic and ego psychology theorists (Kris, 1952; Kubie, 1958) redefine creativity as an ego or preconscious function and tend to reduce Freud's association between creativity and psychopathology. Modern psychoanalytic approaches of object relations and self psychology have also been applied to creativity. Arieti (1967) describes the creative person as "original . . . free . . . tending to fulfill a longing or search for objects and states of experience or existence not easily found nor easily obtainable." Schlesinger (1980) describes the basic creative act as the gradual "construal" of the subjective self, upon which all later creativity will be based. Thus creativity is strongly linked to self-concept and object relatedness.

Some contemporary psychoanalytic writers see adolescence as a critical period in the development of creativity, noting that the character development of the adolescent is intertwined with creative activity (Giovacchini, 1981). Adolescence and creativity are both hallmarked by great fluidity in defensive operations (Shaw, 1981).

Behaviorists have been inclined not to focus on individual patterns of creativity, but to examine its more universal elements. Skinner (1974) views creative people as producing "original responses" as accidental variations in instrumental behavior. These new, original behaviors are selected and maintained by their reinforcing consequences. Mednick (1962) defines creativity as the formation of unusual association between stimuli and responses. Social learning behaviorists, with their interest in mediating variables between stimulus and response, have increasingly focused on self-regulation and self-reinforcement. Bandura (1978) suggests it is through the capacities to manipulate symbols and to engage in reflective thought that individuals generate novel ideas and fashion new environments for self and others.

Humanistic psychology has long posited that each individual has the potential to be highly creative (Rogers, 1954). Maslow (1968) distinguishes between the personal creativity of ordinary people and the creative "products" of artists and scientists. The former is called special talent creativeness; the latter self-actualizing creativeness. What is common between the two is the ability to resolve dichotomies and polarities and to synthesize them into meaningful wholes.

In recent years, neuropsychological researchers have attempted to link high creativity with certain types of neuropsychological organization. Particularly, the pattern of strong right-hemispheric lateralization or dominance, "right-brain," has been associated with originality and creative thinking (Falcone & Loder, 1984; Jausovec, 1983; Katz, 1983; Newland, 1981). "Right-brain" functioning is viewed from this model as more based in synthesis, imagery, metaphor, and emotion (Sinatra, 1984). Efforts to facilitate or develop this neuropsychological organization pattern in children and adults are ongoing but to date evidence is not conclusive.

Creativity and Personality

As well as possessing intellectual or cognitive factors, creativity
has been commonly associated with personality and emotional factors. The ancient Greeks talked of the link between frenzied inspiration and madness, both being disruptions from the conventional order. This correlation of creativity and abnormal personality was
reintroduced in the late nineteenth and early twentieth centuries
(Freud, 1913; Kretschmer, 1931; Lange-Eichbaum, 19832; Lombrosco, 1985). However, during this same period other writers note
no evidence for associating creativity and psychopathology (Ellis,
1904; White, 1938). This pattern of mixed results continues into the
current day. Researchers studying creative individuals within clinical settings and models seem more likely to find associations between creativity and general or specific pathology (Rubenstein &
Levitt, 1980; Slaff, 1981). Those scientists studying nonclinical
groups of creative people utilizing correlation or group designs generally find no systematic relationship, or a small positive relationship between adjustment and creativity (Gupta, 1982; Kakas, 1981;
Paget, 1982; Singh, 1981).

There appear to be important personality factors differentiating
the highly creative from the less creative. Personality traits associated with creativity include high needs for achievement and independence, high persistence, self-reliance, and a sense of personal
responsibility (Albert, 1980). While introversion is often noted as a
characteristic of creative individuals (Baba, 1983; Kumar, 1978;
Marinkovic, 1981), some researchers find correlation between ex-
troversion and creativity (Agarwal & Bohra, 1982; Srinivasan,
1984). On balance, a fairly positive loading of personality factors is
usually ascribed to the creative: intelligent, hard working, willing to
take risks, innovative, independent, sensitive, self-accepting, toler-
ant of ambiguity, enthusiastic.

Albert (1980) states:

> It is clearly in the *emotional* domain that creative persons are
> most distinctive from equally intelligent but less creative con-
> trols — showing unusual ability to withstand long periods of
> loneliness, tension, and emotional strain while in pursuit of
> interests and careers. They rarely become severely psycholog-
> ically ill. Creative persons . . . often exhibit an explicit sense
> of responsibility . . . They are rarely as irresponsible or im-

pulsive as described in popular literature. In none of the above does one find justification for instability, irresponsibility, and bizarreness. (p. 738)

In sum, the study of creativity, as the general field of psychology, is witnessing a growing eclecticism of theory and methods. Historically, researchers were prone to reduce creativity to *either* intellectual *or* personality determinants. Attempts are ongoing to break down such false dichotomies and study creativity more wholistically. Cognitive-style researchers are perhaps the best representatives of this merging of intellectual and emotional perspectives (Gallagher, 1975; Golden, 1975; Noppe & Gallagher, 1977; Rothenberg, 1976). An increasing consensus of scientists views creativity as a cognitive-emotional-behavioral pattern of originality, perseverance, and sustained competence.

THE CREATIVE INDIVIDUAL IN PSYCHOTHERAPY

Despite the generally high level of adjustment evidenced by creative individuals, a certain number of them seek or are referred for psychotherapy. While an accurate census of these persons is lacking, their presence is inferred through a long-standing and growing clinical literature.

Modern psychotherapy research examines the relationships among patient variables, therapy variables, and therapist variables. Seemingly, the key ingredients in understanding psychotherapy with creative individuals are the creative patient, therapy models and techniques, and the therapist.

Patient Variables

It is virtually impossible to define the "typical" creative patient. However, certain characteristics are often brought into therapy by the creative. Characteristics likely to aid therapy include above average intelligence, high achievement, innovativeness, persistence, cognitive complexity, divergent thinking, sensitivity, and tolerance of ambiguity. Other characteristics, however, such as high need to know, need to be independent, questioning authority and technique, and a possible need to control therapy proceedings increase the difficulty of working with creative patients.

Rather than focus on the multitude of manifestations of individual creativity, I would like to examine three *common* profiles or patterns representative of creative individuals in psychotherapy: (1) the creating individual at odds with his or her environment, (2) thwarted creativity, and (3) creativity with severe psychopathology.

The Creating Individual at Odds with Environment

Even in the absence of major psychopathology creative people may, particularly to others, appear work-obsessed, moody, and unempathic. Albert (1980) writes:

> Such a constellation [creativity] often puts a strain on creative persons internally and creates cleavage between them and some significant part of their environment. It is not surprising to find that creative persons *are* tense, irritable, and "pulled in" while engaged in creative operations. (p. 738)

This sense of mission and commitment to extended, often isolated, task performance is often a strain to family and friends. While generally not equivalent to clinical obsession (Binik, Fainsilber & Spevack, 1981), this preoccupation with internal, personal pursuits may cause or exacerbate relationship problems. This feature of disequilibrium or imbalance is noted by Sarnoff and Cole (1983), who maintain that the channeling of creativity into production has distanced individuals from nonrational aspects of their being, leading them to feelings of alienation and anomie. Additionally, there may be conflict within the creative individual regarding balancing work and relationships. The following case vignette affords a view of this pattern of creativity.

> Ms. S. was a self-referred 25-year-old single female with no previous psychiatric history. She had excelled at ballet from an early age and was currently a lead dancer with a major ballet company. The eldest daughter of two artistic parents, she had seen and experienced the continual conflict of her parents, particularly her mother, between parenting and pursuing an artistic career. She reported similar conflicts, noting that her career had forced her to end several relationships. More than one man had described her as "career obsessed" and

"incapable of intimacy." She currently was in love with a man and wished to continue both the relationship and her career.

Thwarted Creativity

A certain number of creative persons report episodic or protracted blocks in expressing their talents, often described as "writer's block" or "performance anxiety." What seems to develop in the person whose creativity is thwarted or blocked is a vicious circle of negative attitude and expectancies (loss of confidence), loaded emotionality (anxiety and depression, and task-avoidant behavior. The result is an individual who wants desperately to create but can't, experiencing ever increasing frustration and pessimism. Usually this type of patient enters psychotherapy as a last resort, having exhausted a variety of self-treatments. The following case vignette illustrates this type of problem.

> Ms. M. was a physician-referred 31-year-old single female. She had been in psychotherapy previously (five years ago) for anxiety problems. She had reported some improvement but had noted a progressive reappearance of anxiety symptoms and other psychological problems. The patient was an established writer whose previous work had been published and adapted for television. For the last two years she had been unsuccessfully working on a major play. She reported being "blocked." She felt her writing skills had deteriorated and evidenced increasing patterns of anxiety, depression, task avoidance, and social isolation.

Creativity with Severe Psychopathology

While the myth of crazed genius is generally not supported, certain creative persons do express both creativity and serious psychopathology. This pathology can run the gamut from circumscribed and mild to pervasive and major. The following is a case where creativity coexists with a severe personality disorder.

> Mr. S. was a physician-referred 37-year-old divorced male. The patient presented as moderately depressed, ruminative, and confused. He had experienced a series of interpersonal losses over a two year period: death of mother, divorce from

wife and son, and end of a heterosexual dating relationship. Previous treatment had included antidepressant medication and supportive counseling. Mr. S. described lifelong feelings of emptiness and long-standing conflict with his family. The patient had been a television entertainer as a child. As an adult, he still performed throughout the country in stage musicals, live and televised variety shows, and concerts. He reported feeling at ease and in control while on stage, but empty, depressed, and confused when not performing.

Table 1 outlines general therapeutic issues with these three common creativity patterns.

THERAPY VARIABLES

Some creative individuals may view psychotherapy as dangerous, a vehicle for stripping them of their originality (Fine, 1984). It, therefore, may be important for the therapist to explicitly state and reinforce the idea that psychotherapy offers the general goal of re-translating and *expanding* an individual's qualities of action, thought, and affect (Dunn, 1985). The movement of most schools of therapy away from procrustean, overly dogmatic procedures should aid in allaying possible patient anxiety regarding loss of creativity. An explicit, collaborative, flexible therapeutic approach also serves to reduce negative transference, countertransference, and resistance issues.

While there are a wide variety of psychotherapy models, therapy's central stance is usually defined as one of the following: treatment of pathology, adjustment, or self-actualization. Each of these three stances can be helpful, effective reference points for therapy with creative patients. The degree of patient psychopathology is likely the single best indicator of which therapeutic stance to employ. In the absence of significant pathology, an adjustment or self-actualizing approach would seem to mesh best with the constellation of creative attributes. The presence of severe pathology, on the other hand, necessitates treatment as a major goal and reduces the utilization of therapeutic process or techniques predicated on reasonable patient adjustment or high ego strength.

Table 1

Patterns of Creativity and Psychotherapy

Creativity Pattern	Patient Sense of Self	Clinical Observations	Goals of Psychotherapy
The Creating Individual At Odds With Environment	Preoccupied with creative task Pressured, frustrated, annoyed at task-diverting people and situations Experienced and/or expressed guilt and anxiety over creative preoccupation	No major past or current psychopathology evidenced by patient Patient's creative preoccupation results in lower quality relating in other life pursuits Evidence of dichotomous, "black & white" thinking regarding life choices (e.g., "I'm either creating or not")	Resolution of conflict with significant others Development of a variety of non-dichotomous alternatives in thought & behavior serving to integrate patient's creative activity with other roles and obligations
Thwarted Creativity	Increasing inability to express creativity Preoccupation with lack of creative accomplishment and feelings of failure, anticipatory & performance anxiety, and depression	No severe psychopathology prior to current situation Current situation may exacerbate pre-existing mild to moderate psychopathology Discernible emergence of "vicious cycle" regarding creativity -lack of productivity -loss of confidence -task avoidance -increased negative affect	Breaking Vicious Cycle -Anxiety/depression Management -Increasing creative task involvement -Cognitive restructuring -Addressing diminished sense of self
Creativity with Severe Psychopathology	Depending upon type of pathology, patient's sense of self may be underdeveloped, punitive, distorted, or fragmented	Observable pattern of significant past & current psychopathology Creativity expressed along with severe intrapsychic and/or interpersonal problems	Treatment of psychopathology Subsequent integration of patient's creativity with "healthier self"

Techniques

A diversity of psychotherapy techniques have been advocated for use with creative patients. These include use of patient's dreams and fantasies (Fisher, 1981), use of patient's writing and articulation (Hoffman & Lewis, 1981; Rothenberg, 1983), imagery and metaphor (Ostrom, 1981), paradox (Henning, 1981), and hypothesis-testing and homospatial thinking (Rothenberg, 1984).

The large number and variety of techniques employed with some success suggest that a single technique or specific sequence of techniques is probably not the essential element of successful effective therapy with the creative. It would seem that a variety of techniques may be useful as aids or adjuncts to the main therapeutic process of adjustment, self-actualization or treatment of pathology. The importance of techniques which provide the patient with information (vs. control) has been stressed (Koestner, Ryan, Bernieri, & Holt, 1984). This is consonant with the view of creative individuals as forming and using their own psychological structures and meanings, not borrowing those of others.

Tasks of Psychotherapy

Across theoretical perspectives, successful psychotherapy is hallmarked by accurate assessment, establishing a therapeutic alliance, and focusing on selective goals and objectives via a therapeutic contract (Dunn, 1985). Each of these activities or tasks offers the therapist an opportunity to increase his or her understanding and treatment efficacy regarding the creative patient.

Assessment

The therapist and patient mutually explore patient history, symptoms, and phenomenology. Of particular concern to therapy with the creative are which pattern of creativity is expressed and the type and severity of any coexisting psychopathology.

Therapeutic Alliance

The therapist facilitates a respectful, accepting milieu in which the patient can reduce defensiveness, explore self-knowledge and change. The emphasis on collaboration, activity and flexibility would be especially important in working with creative persons.

Therapeutic Contract

A mutual "frame of reference" is formulated in accord with patient, therapy, and therapist variables. This results in a contract specific to an individual patient. With most creative patients, this contract needs to represent a dynamic structure, more of a reference point than a constraining structure. Increased patient psychopathology, as stated, would necessitate greater emphasis on an explicit, higher structure, symptom-related contract.

Therapist Variables

Regardless of theoretical models and techniques, a therapist's "self" is an essential ingredient in psychotherapy and may be the key to successfully working with creative patients. Fisher (1981) sees the therapist's function with these type of patients as engendering a sense of spontaneous, integrated wholeness. As well, the therapist needs to move with the patient toward the "valuable and new" (Rothenberg, 1984). Quaytman (1976) suggests the therapist utilize diverse approaches and avoid dogma.

What emerges, unsurprisingly, is a portrait of a therapist who possesses nonspecific therapeutic skills (empathy, genuineness, and warmth), is active, nondefensive, collaborative, flexible in treatment, but comfortable in asserting necessary structure (e.g., rigorous assessment, techniques, contract). Table 2 summarizes the major tasks of therapy regarding the three patients introduced in preceding vignettes. While the same basic therapeutic tasks exist in each case, the variety and individuality of treatment should be noted.

Arieti (1967) states that a central feature of the creative process is the individual's ability to "concretize" an abstract concept in the form of a multidimensional metaphor. This metaphor (e.g., use of the double helix to represent DNA structure; use of seasons to represent the lifespan) serves as an anchor for creative intrapsychic exploration and as a vehicle for information exchange with others. The metaphor is dynamic, that is, capable of further articulation by both logical and perceptive psychological processes. Elements of knowledge are synthesized into meaningful wholes.

This also may relate to what Schlesinger (1980) describes as "construal," a mental construction process by which an individual integrates experiential and cognitive-behavioral self-information

Table 2

Psychotherapy With Creative Patients - Three Cases

Therapy Task	Ms. S.	Ms. M.	Mr. S.
Assessment			
Patient's Self-Assessment	"My career & personal life are in conflict."	"I'm emotionally unable to write."	"I am empty."
Therapist's Assessment	Absence of significant pre-morbid psychopathology Ongoing & increasing anxiety surrounding life choice issues	Moderate dysthymic disorder Moderate clinical anxiety "Vicious Cycle" regarding creative process	Severe dysthymic disorder Mixed personality disorder
Creativity Pattern	Creativity at odds with Environment	Thwarted creativity	Creativity and severe psychopathology
Alliance			
General Therapeutic Stance	Therapist encourages exploration & integration of work & relationship roles vs. choosing one over the other	Therapist encourages alternatives to and reduction of punitive self-evaluation & "vicious cycle." Expression/exploration of anxious & depressive affect	Therapist encourages the mourning of losses & the building of a broader, deeper base of self-knowledge.
Contract			
Patient's Perspective	Help in choosing career & relationship options	Less depression & more productivity	Less depression & emptiness
Therapist's Perspective	Creative combining of career & relationship goals	Breaking "vicious cycle" Anxiety & depression reduction	Development of a personalized self-concept
Therapy Process			
	Attachment Exploration of conflicting roles Integration vs. dichotinization of roles Attitudinal changes toward roles via cognitive restructuring & mutual problem solving	Attachment Exploration of patient's phenomenology Enhanced patient control via reduced negative affect & enhanced, less conditional sense of self	Attachment Grieving for losses Reduced depression & emptiness via patient internalization of attributes, skills, & values into consistent values, self-concept

27

into meaningful metaphors, concepts, and patterns. This process is seen as the basis for self-understanding and effective object relations.

We might view therapy with the creative as a process in which, initially, an "entrance self-metaphor" is generated, representative of the patient's current complaint or pathology. Subsequently, therapy either reconstructs this dysfunctional self-metaphor or, in some cases, constructs an alternative metaphor from the patient's ongoing life experience. This revised or new metaphor becomes a therapeutic focus, a loom on which therapist and patient weave a more fully articulated and understood pattern of patient perception, cognition, and behavior, using both retrospective analysis of life events and "here and now" experiencing of therapeutic process.

Brief therapy with patients usually works at the periphery of self (behavior, thought, relationships). Therapist and patient construct a self-metaphor representative of patient attitudes, roles, and behaviors with which to understand and aid interpersonal relations and environmental coping (e.g., Ms. S.).

Longer term treatment entails a more subjective self-metaphor (deep beliefs, emotions, perceptions), constructed from the patient's core cognitive-affective schematae. Transactional or process elements of therapy play an increased role in constructing and embellishing a more experiential self-metaphor. As noted this "construal" task may involve enhancing or integrating an existing dysfunctional metaphor (e.g., Ms. M.) or construction of a new healthier one (e.g., Mr. S.).

Major tasks of the therapist are to: (a) collaborate with the creative patient in the construction of a *mutually understandable and useful* self-metaphor at a depth consonant with therapy parameters, and (b) guide therapy content and process toward the embellishment and greater understanding of this dynamic central metaphor. Particularly in longer term therapy the therapist uses techniques and process to keep the self-metaphor perceptually vivid so as to aid in its ongoing accessibility and internalization. Metaphors should arise from the unique process and content of each case, rather than being imposed by the therapist from a preexisting list.

Table 3 notes the dysfunctional "entrance self-metaphors" evidenced by the aforementioned three patients. The more functional self-metaphors established in therapy are also included. A variety of nonspecific and specific therapy skills and techniques (e.g., imagery, role-playing, homework assignments, clarification, cognitive

Table 3

Self-Metaphors and Psychotherapy – A Comparison of Three Cases

	Ms. S	Ms. M.	Mr. S
Entrance Complaint	Role Conflict – Self seen as alternating between two incompatible & dichatomous personae	Thwarted Creativity – Self seen as diminished due to lack of creative output	Emptiness – Self seen as a performer without a personalized psychological interior
Dysfunctional Entrance Self-Metaphor	Two-Headed Bust of Self	Two-dimensional black & white portrait labeled "Failed Writer"	Blank Sheet of Paper
Therapy-Constructed Self Metaphor	One-Headed Bust of Self	Three-dimensional, colored self-image labeled "Self Portrait"	Character Sketch of "Self"
Therapy Metaphor Representative of:	Integration of conflicting roles into a single self role containing some qualities of each	An expanded, deepened sense of self awareness & competency	Establishment of beliefs, values, & internal dialogue & other elements of an individualized self-identity

29

restructuring, relaxation, utilization of process) were used to aid the process of metaphor construction and utilization.

In most cases, therapy focuses on the elaboration of a single central self-metaphor. However, particularly in longer term therapy, a self-metaphor may be "outgrown" or prove inadequate (e.g., not perceptually vivid; incapable of embellishment). In such instances therapist and patient need to assess the limitations of the current self-metaphor and proceed toward the creation of a more robust, dynamic self-metaphor.

The skill of the therapist lies in assessing the unique blend of resources and deficits brought by the creative individual, conducting therapy at an optimal depth in terms of self-metaphor construction, and, mindful of the patient's limits and pathology, allowing that patient to bring his or her creativity to bear on the therapeutic process.

REFERENCES

Agarwal, S., & Bohra, S. (1982). Study of personality pattern of high and low creative children. *Child Psychiatry Quarterly, 15*(4), 136-139.

Albert, R. (1980). Genius. In R. Woody (Ed.), *Encyclopedia of Clinical Assessment* (pp. 729-743). San Francisco: Jossey-Bass.

Alpaugh, P., & Birren, J. (1975). Are there sex differences in creativity across the adult life span? *Human Development, 188*, 461-465.

Anastasi, A., & Schaefer, C. (1971). Note on the concepts of creativity and intelligence. *Journal of Creative Behavior, 5*, 113-116.

Arieti, S. (1967). *The intrapsychic self: Feeling, cognition, and creativity in health and mental health.* New York: Basic Books.

Baba, Y. (1983). Social adaptability of high, medium, and low creative persons as assessed by human figure image tests. *Japanese Journal of Psychology, 53*(6), 358-364.

Bandura, A. (1978). The self-system in reciprocal determination. *American Psychologist, 33*, 344-358.

Barron, F. (1969). *Creative person and creative process.* New York: Holt, Rinehart, & Winston.

Binik, Y., Fainsilber, L., & Spevack, M. (1981). Obsessionality and creativity. *Canadian Journal of Behavioral Science, 13*(1), 25-32.

Cattell, R., & Butcher, H. (1968). *The prediction of achievement and creativity.* New York: Bobbs-Merrill.

Cox, C. (1926). *Genetic studies of genius*, (Vol. 2). Stanford, CA: Stanford University Press.

Dacey, J. (1982). *Adult development.* Glenview, IL: Scott, Foresman.

Dunn, R. (1985). Issues of self-concept deficit in psychotherapy. *Psychotherapy, 22*(4), 747-751.

Ellis, H. (1904). *A study of British genius.* London: Hurt & Blackett.

Falcone, D., & Loder, K. (1984). A modified lateral eye-movement measure, the right hemisphere and creativity left gaze and upward gaze for Uses Test. *Perceptual and Motor Skills, 58*(3), 823-830.

Fine, R. (1984). The effect of psychoanalysis on the creative individual. *Current Issues in Psychoanalytic Practice, 1*(1), 3-28.

Fisher, S. (1981). Some observations on psychotherapy and creativity. *Adolescent Psychiatry, 9,* 528-538.

Freud, S. (1913). *Leonardo da Vinci: A study in sexuality.* New York: Random House.

Gallagher, J. (1975). *Teaching the gifted child.* Boston: Allyn & Bacon.

Galton, R. (1869). *Hereditary genius: An inquiry into its laws and consequences.* New York: Macmillan.

Getzels, J., & Csikszentmihalyi, M. (1975). From problem solving to problem finding. In I. Taylor & J. Getzels (Eds.), *Perspectives in Creativity* (pp. 90-116). Chicago: Aldine.

Giovacchine, P. (1981). Creativity, adolescence, and inevitable failure. *Adolescent Psychiatry, 99,* 35-39.

Golden, C. (1975). The measurement of creativity by the Stroop Color and Word Test. *Journal of Personality Assessment, 39,* 502-506.

Guilford, J. (1971). Some misconceptions regarding measurement of creative talents. *Journal of Creative Behavior, 5*(2), 77-87.

Guilford, J. (1984). Varieties of divergent production. *Journal of Creative Behavior, 18*(1), 1-10.

Gupta, G. (1982). Creativity and adjustment at various educational levels. *Indian Psychological Review, 23,* 16-19.

Henning, L. (1981). Paradox as a treatment for writer's block. *Personnel & Guidance Journal, 60*(2), 112-113.

Hoffman, A., & Lewis, N. (1981). The needle of caring, the thread of love: Creative writing on an adolescent medical ward. *Adolescent Psychiatry, 99,* 88-116.

Ihanus, J. (1982). Freud and the fruits of the realm of fantasy. (Finn) *Psykologia, 17*(4), 257-262.

Jaques, E. (1964). Death and the midlife crisis. *International Journal of Psychoanalysis, 46,* 502-514.

Jausovec, N. (1983). The relationship between age, hemisphericity & creativity. (Sloe) *Anthropos,* Nos. 5-6, 185-195.

Kagan, J. (1984). *The nature of the child.* New York: Basic Books.

Kakas, G. (1981). A study on the connections between creativity and frustration tolerance. (Hung) *Magyar Pszichologiai Szemle, 38*(1), 23-29.

Katz, A. (1983). Creativity and individual differences in asymmetric cerebral hemispheric functioning. *Empirical Studies of the Arts, 1*(1), 3-16.

Koestner, R., Ryan, R., Bernieri, F., & Holt, K. (1984). Setting limits on children's behavior: The differential effects of controlling vs. informational styles on intrinsic motivation & creativity. *Journal of Personality, 52,* 233-248.

Kretschmer, E. (1931). *The psychology of men of genius.* New York: Harcourt, Brace, Jovanovich.

Kris, E. (1952). *Psychoanalytic explorations in art.* New York: International Universities Press.

Kubie, L. (1958). *Neurotic distortion of the creative process*. Lawrence, KS: University of Kansas Press.

Kumar, G. (1978). Creativity functioning in relation to personality, value-orientation, and achievement motivation. *Indian Educational Review, 13*(2), 110-115.

Lange-Eichbaum, W. (1932). *The problem of genius*. New York: MacMillan.

Lombrosco, C. (1895). *The man of genius*. New York: Scribner's.

Marinkovic, M. (1981). Importance of introversion for science and creativity. (Germ) *Analytische Psychologie, 12*(1), 1-35.

Maslow, A. (1968). *Toward a psychology of being*, (2nd ed.). New York: Van Nostrand Reinhold Co.

Mednick, S. (1962). The associative basis of the creative process. *Psychological Review, 699*, 220-232.

Newland, G. (1981). Differences between left and right-handers on a measure of creativity. *Perceptual and Motor Skills, 53*(3), 787-792.

Noppe, L., & Gallagher, J. (1977). A cognitive style approach to creative thought. *Journal of Personality Assessment, 41*, 85-90.

Ostrom, G. (1981). Imagery and intuition: Keys to counseling the gifted, talented, and creative. *Creative Child and Adult Quarterly, 6*(4), 227-233.

Paget, K. (1982). The creative abilities of children with social and emotional problems. *Journal of Abnormal Child Psychology, 10*(1), 107-111.

Pressy, S. (1949). *Educational acceleration: Appraisals and basic problems*. Columbus, OH: Ohio University Press.

Quaytman, W. (1976). What makes a creative psychotherapist. In A. Banet (Ed.), *Creative Psychotherapy* (pp. 77-81). La Jolla, CA: University Associates.

Rogers, C. (1954). Toward a theory of creativity. *ETC: A Review of General Semantics, 11*, 249-260.

Rothenberg, A. (1976). Janusian thinking and creativity. In W. Meunsterberger, A. Esman, & L. Boyer (Eds.), *The psychoanalytic study of society* (pp. 1-30). New Haven, CT: Yale University Press.

Rothenberg, A. (1983). Creativity, articulation, and psychotherapy. *Journal of the American Academy of Psychoanalysis, 11*(1), 55-85.

Rothenberg, A. (1984). Creativity & psychotherapy. *Psychoanalysis and Contemporary Thought, 7*(21), 233-268.

Rubenstein, B., & Levitt, M. (1980). The creative process and the narcissistic personality disorder. *International Journal of Psychoanalytic Psychotherapy, 88*, 461-482.

Sarnoff, D., & Cole, H. (1983). Creativity and personal growth. *Journal of Creative Behavior, 17*(2), 95-102.

Schlesinger, K. (1980). On the creative process and the human capacity to construe. *International Journal of Psychoanalytic Psychotherapy, 88*, 483-500.

Schmukler, D. (1982). A factor analytic model of elements of creativity in preschool children. *Genetic Psychology Monographs, 105*(1), 25-39.

Shaw, J. (1981). Adolescence, mourning, and creativity. *Adolescent Psychiatry, 9*, 60-67.

• Sinatra, R. (1984). Brain functioning & creative behavior. *Roeper Review, 7*(1), 48-54.

Singh, R. (1981). Creativity in relation to adjustment. *Psychological Studies, 26*(2), 84-85.

Skinner, B. F. (1974). *About behaviorism.* New York: Alfred A. Knopf.

Slaff, B. (1981). Creativity: Blessing or burden? *Adolescent Psychology, 99,* 78-87.

Srinivasan, T. (1984). Originality in relation to extraversion, introversion, neuroticism, & psychoticism. *Journal of Psychological Researches, 28*(2), 65-70.

Terman, L. (1925). *Genetic studies of genius* (Vol. 1). Stanford, CA: University Press.

Torrance, E. (1971). Psychology of gifted children and youth. In W. M. Cruickshank (Ed.), *Psychology of exceptional children and youth* (3rd ed.) (pp. 528-564). Englewood Cliffs, NJ: Prentice-Hall.

White, R. (1930). Note on the psychopathology of genius. *Journal of Social Psychology, 1,* 311-315.

Psychotherapy as a Creative Process

Robert D. Romanyshyn

SUMMARY. Through a consideration of a case history psychotherapy is described as a creative process consisting of the moment of landscaping, figuring, and storying experience. Special emphasis is placed upon the work of re-membering in this creative process and final consideration is given to how this approach to psychotherapy regards the issues of symptoms and dreams.

INTRODUCTION

Diane was a 26-year-old woman who came to see me because of her inability to make choices about the directions of her life. Specifically, she could not decide whether she should marry Leonard, the man with whom she had been living for several years, or return to San Francisco where her parents lived in order to pursue a degree in creative writing. She did not see the two choices as mutually exclusive. It was possible, she thought, to marry and to relocate. Leonard had applied for a position in San Francisco which he honestly wanted, but there was some chance that he would have to locate elsewhere. In the latter case, should she follow him and give up her acceptance into the creative-writing program she so ardently desired? Or should she end the relationship and enter the program? Unable to decide, she waited and hoped for circumstances to make the decision for her. Every day she would awake and postpone a decision, hoping that Leonard would get the job in San Francisco.

Robert D. Romanyshyn is Professor of Psychology at the University of Dallas and Visiting Professor in Humanities at the University of Texas at Dallas. He has lectured widely in the U.S., Europe, and Africa. Author of *Psychological Life: From Science to Metaphor*, he has recently finished a book on nuclear culture entitled *In the Shadow of the Bomb: Technology as Symptom and Dream*. At the present time he is also working on a book on psychotherapy entitled *Notes of a Witness*. Mailing address: University of Dallas, 1845 E. Northgate, Irving, TX 75062.

That would solve everything: They could relocate together and be married; she would be near her parents again; and she could begin her career as a writing student.

But as the days went by and stretched into weeks Diane began to panic. The deadline for her decision about school was getting close and Leonard still had received no word. In desperation she telephoned for an appointment, hoping, as she made clear in the first hour, that I could tell her what was the best thing to do. She came for advice. If circumstances would not make the choice for her, then perhaps someone else (the psychotherapist) could and would do so.

The situation which I have just described is certainly not extraordinary. Psychotherapists encounter it in one form or another on a frequent and even regular basis. But as often as I encounter it I am reminded of how very fragile is the initial bond between therapist and patient. The patient comes looking for direction. One enters psychotherapy with a hope that the therapist will give the right advice, or remove the symptom, or save the marriage, or make one happy — or some such variation on the theme. The patient comes, in other words, willing and even wanting to give over responsibility for his or her life to the therapist, and as Guggenbuhl-Craig (1976) so clearly describes, the therapist, out of his or her own needs to be flattered or to be seen as a saviour or a prophet or at least a good therapist, can easily take over that proffered responsibility. But psychotherapy is no more a giving of advice and direction than it is a prescription for happiness. It is not even primarily concerned with the *removal* of symptoms. On the contrary, as I hope to show here, psychotherapy is a creative process that allows the patient to take up responsibility for his or her own life. In less formal terms psychotherapy as a creative process is a matter of making a space and creating a mood wherein the events of a life are re-figured as stories. Taking up responsibility for one's life means that the patient within this space takes up the task of re-working events into experiences. One engages in that work which Rank (1959) called the "volitional affirmation of the obligatory" (p. 164) and which he saw as not only therapeutically useful but also as definitely creative. Or to draw upon the thought of that sadly neglected Spanish philosopher, Ortega y Gasset (Marias, 1970), the patient makes the circumstances of life a vocation, and called out by these circumstances, the events and relations which surround one, the patient begins the work of re-fashioning the details of a life into a work. As a creative process, then, psychotherapy opens up a space wherein the patient begins the art of living life as art, and in this process of re-membering what has already been given, comes to recognize the truth which the poet Eliot (1971, p. 59) knew when he wrote:

> . . . And the end of all our exploring
> Will be to arrive where we started
> And know the place for the first time.

Through the case of Diane I want to describe what I will call the three moments of the creative process of psychotherapy: the moments of landscaping, figuring, and storying experience. These moments will then take us into a consideration of how the work of re-membering is a key part of this creative process. In the conclusion I will consider how this focus on psychotherapy as a work of creation changes one's regard for what is a symptom and what is a dream. Symptom and dream become the basic material, "prima materia," for this work of creative re-membering.

MOMENTS IN THE CREATIVE PROCESS:
THE CASE OF DIANE

To listen to a patient is initially to wonder *who* is speaking. Indeed this is perhaps the first question for the therapist without which one is likely to assume that it is the *person* of the patient who speaks. Such an assumption, however, would be erroneous and finally also detrimental to psychotherapy as a creative process. Initially, therefore, the therapist must practice that kind of attitude which the poet-philosopher Samuel Taylor Coleridge (1968) described for those who would believe in the poetic creations of the imagination. The therapist must adopt a "willing suspension of disbelief" (p. 274) which allows one to hear beneath the content of the patient's words its characterization. A tale is being told and the task of the therapist is to listen for the *figure* who tells the tale, for the figure who is spinning the story.

Person and figure are related to each other in much the same way that an actor is related to the character portrayed. When I watch Dustin Hoffman, for example, play the part of Willie Loman, I see and hear the character of Willie and not the person of Dustin Hoffman who portrays him. The actor here *is* the character he displays and if this is not the case then I am exiled from the world of Willie, barred from hearing his tale. On the other hand, however, I know all the while that the character of Willie Loman lives through the person of an actor; and I even know that here in this case it is the actor Hoffman who brings to the role a decidedly different configuration than that brought to it by Lee J. Cobb's or Frederick March's portrayals. I know all of this and yet again I see Willie Loman. In the darkness and silence of the theater, within the mood created by the space of the stage, I practice that Coleridgean suspension of disbelief. Indeed it is perhaps even more correct to say that this suspension of disbelief happens rather than that I practice it. It simply happens that my knowledge gives way to a belief which ushers me across a threshold and escorts me into the presence of Willie Loman. In spite of what I know I do not doubt that there before me appears and speaks the figure of the dying salesman.

Diane's indecisiveness and the anxiety attendant upon it was given through her voice and her posture, and as I listened to that voice and noticed that posture the person of Diane began to flesh out before me a figure. Her voice was really remarkable and even in the first hour I could not help but notice its soft, tremulous quality. It was a voice which sounded young and filled with quiet tears. In the space of my office we were never more than 10 feet apart, but I often found myself leaning in, as it were, to catch what she was saying. Whoever was here before me, whoever was speaking, was far away. The person of Diane was there with me in the neutral space of my office, the space which is the same for all my patients. But the figure who was speaking transformed that space into another world. Through the quality of her voice my patient was telling me that she inhabited a different space, a space which on one hand I felt I had to lean into and which on the other hand seemed so distant and far away. In the first few hours, then, I listened to that voice and I wondered who was speaking. But I also waited in order to become more familiar with its character. A therapist can become too impatient here, too quick to assume one knows who is speaking. One must wait, therefore, to be touched and/or moved by the figure. One must allow oneself to be addressed.

Diane sat on the sofa in such a way that her posture complemented the character of her voice. She invariably curled up into a corner, tucking her legs beneath her and arching her shoulders and head into her chest. Because she was rather small to begin with and also rather thin and fragile in appearance, the posture she adopted made her appear even smaller, and indeed almost tiny. I would look at her across the room and her posture would mirror back to me how straight and how solid was my own sitting, and I would feel a certain incongruity between us. Diane's posture was creating a space around her; in the way she sat she was making a space, a space of enclosure. Reflected through that space I began to recognize that by contrast I was only in space. I had not yet entered the space which the figure of Diane inhabited, and the distance which the quality of her voice announced was re-affirmed by the difference between our styles of incarnation. Through her body the figure whose voice sounded so young and filled with tears was setting the stage for her experience, and it was only in my own initial vague bodily sense of leaning in that my own posture began to resonate with that of my patient. Leaning in was a muscular acknowledgement of who was speaking, and it indicated that before I knew who was speaking my body knew it. Leaning in, I was no longer just a body in space, the therapist sitting in his chair across the room from his patient, but a body making its space, participating with the patient in the creation of a landscape.

The person of Diane was in my office, but the figure who was speaking dwells within a landscape. Just as a character belongs to a stage, a figure inhabits a landscape; and Diane's voice and posture announced both who was speaking and the place from where she spoke. The distance and postural difference that were initially felt by me proclaimed that the one who was speaking was a young girl, perhaps no more than five years of age, who spoke from within a space of enclosure. The distant character of her voice *was* the youth. The young girl who was speaking announced herself in sounding so enclosed and so far away. In hearing the distance I heard someone who belonged to another time and who was speaking now here in my office across that space of time. Through the character of the voice and the posture of the body, then, the patient presented the figure she was. Through them she created within the setting of my office the young girl enclosed within her space.

To be sure there was a content being spoken throughout these first few hours. Characters on stage have their lines. They enact a drama. They tell a story. A patient's tale, however, differs in an important way from the tale told by a character whom an actor portrays. The metaphor of therapy as theater which has so far marked my presentation indicates a difference as well as an identity between theater and therapy. The difference is that the patient is making the story as she or he enacts it. The drama is being written as it is being performed. The story that is spoken in therapy is woven together out of the odds and ends, the bits and pieces, the small hurts and otherwise incidental occurrences which compose the fabric of a life. The moments of landscaping, figuring, and storying experience are a work of re-membering.

MAKING A STORY/RE-MEMBERING A PAST

Her room, she said, was her sanctuary. It was, when she was a little girl, a place of retreat. Not only a retreat, however, into safety; her room was also a retreat into fantasy and daydream. She would go there to escape the criticisms of mother and in that space she would dream about her father. She loved him intensely and she knew that if she only could be a person she could care for him better than her mother did. But he always seemed distant and preoccupied. He always seemed sad and she worried that her need to be loved by him might only be another burden.

Diane would speak these words and others like them in that soft, trembling voice, curled up in one corner of the couch; and it was not difficult to imagine that she was creating in the enclosed space of safety and dreams from which to speak a variation of her childhood room. At times there would be long periods of silence and/or quiet tears, and on occasion she would shudder as if she was cold. Noticing this reaction, I asked her once if she was cold and what she needed to be warm again. Her reply was not verbal. Rather she took the comforter which blanketed the couch and the several pillows located in the therapy room and built a kind of shelter. It was, she said, a cave and in there she could be warm while the world outside was ice. For the next several months Diane would begin each hour with this ritual of building the cave and from that space she would speak about her childhood memories and her current fantasies and dreams. And always in one guise or another father would appear in her words: father as absent but in need of her, or father as hurt or sick and longing for the presence of his daughter. But it would never happen. Father would never come and Diane would remain in her cave-room-enclosed space, silent, longing, tearful, and young.

In the beginning of our work this recognition would leave Diane silent or in tears, but as our time together lengthened she began to voice some disappointment and then some anger. She also became increasingly angry with me. I had already mentioned on several occasions that I had to lean in in order to hear her speak from within the cave, and on occasion I even had to move my chair a few feet closer. But now Diane was challenging me to come to the mouth of her cave. "Are you afraid?" she would demand. "Are you afraid to come here where there is life and heat and fire and blood?" During this period of our work together she also remembered an incident concerning her room, which, however, she was not quite sure actually happened. Her words were as follows: "I once played by myself, in my room. It was an adventure game, a daydream about knights and princesses. I was lying on my bed and my mother came in, and I felt ashamed." This reported memory was shortly followed by a dream in which she and a girlfriend with whom she was always being compared by her mother were doing something bad downstairs. The friend got caught but in the dream Diane escaped upstairs.

Was her remembered room of childhood upstairs? Were her memory of the adventure game and her dream of doing something bad downstairs allusions to childhood sexual experiences and fantasies, particularly in relation to father? Did Diane learn at any early and impressionable age to retreat into passivity and indecisiveness, to escape to the enclosed space of safety and dreams, in order to soften and to silence her own normal but misunderstood erotic desires? Did her father encourage these desires and then draw away? And now was her new challenging attitude toward me a resurrection of these older themes?

It would make a tidy summary to be able to affirm answers to all these questions. Her childhood room as in fact upstairs, but for the rest it is not possible to say with certainty. It is not even possible to affirm that the memory of the adventure game in her room refers to an actual event. Diane herself was vague and unsure. And yet it matters very little here whether Diane told a *factually* accurate story. Commenting on Freud's notion of "psychical reality" the astute critic and observer of psychoanalysis Paul Ricoeur (1978) has noted that "it is not clinically relevant whether the infantile scenes (which the patient remembers in analysis) are true or false." And lest we are misled by the term clinical here, Ricoeur the philosopher adds that "it does not matter, therefore, from an epistemological point of view either" (p. 188). Re-membering the past is not merely a matter of accuracy to be checked and measured against what really was. It is also, and more profoundly so, a matter of intention in light of what one wishes and/or believes oneself to be. In the process of psychotherapy Diane re-membered her past in the light of making a story by which to live. As a consequence of that work she was able to leave therapy. Through the work of re-membering *she* was able to dismantle the cave-room-enclosed space within which she had been living. Re-membering her past, Diane was able to end therapy by leaving her room.

It may appear at this point, however, that, insofar as the work of re-membering has little to do with the discovery of some real but buried factual past, the creative process of psychotherapy borders on the realm of fiction making. But we would be forced toward adopting this view only because, as I have shown elsewhere (Romanyshyn, 1982), psychology is so uncritically allied to the natural sciences that it is difficult to recognize that our image of time as a line, which today, as Rifkin (1984), Capra (1982), and others have shown, is even increasingly questionable to describe the causal relations between events and processes in the physical world and to an even lesser degree in the biological world, is totally inadequate with respect to events and processes in the human psychological world. A phenomenology of human temporal experience (Merleau-Ponty, 1962; Minkowski, 1970; Van den Berg, 1972) demonstrates that between the past and the present there is not a one-way relation of cause and effect but a reciprocal relation of meaning and intention. In short, one's past changes in relation to the present from which one re-members the past and in light of a future which one now intends. The childhood I recall now at 40 or so is not the same childhood I remembered in my 20s. Moreover, it serves us ill here to retreat into the formula that the meaning of the past changes but not the past itself, for what is the past for any individual except that which one is in relation to? For whom would a past in itself exist? It could exist only for one who has neither a present nor a future, that is, only for one who does not live within time.

If, therefore, we base our understanding of the work of re-membering upon the experience of time as we live it, then the creative process of psychotherapy is no more a matter of making fictions that it is a matter of discovering facts. This dichotomy of fact and fiction simply will not work here. It is not an either/or situation. Rather we are led and even forced by the evidence of experience itself to affirm the paradox that the past is something given in order to be made. Re-membering the past is a matter of making a real past real. It is, as I have described it elsewhere (Romanyshyn, 1986), a matter of fictionalizing the factual. In the creative process of psychotherapy, as in life, re-membering is in the root sense of the word a poeticizing, a making or crafting, of one's history.

The paradox of the past as a given to be made, the tension which vibrates in the phrase *fictionalizing the factual*, is more readily understandable when we recognize that in its root sense *fiction* means to form or to mold and that it originally described the process of molding or shaping a clay pot from the earth. As a making, therefore, fiction produces something real. It produces an artifact of the cultural world. Moreover, as a making, fiction works with and reshapes something already given, something already made. It remakes the given earth. In its original sense, in the story of an experience which the word fiction describes, the work of fictionalizing is simultaneously the *transformation* and *preservation* of the earth. The clay pot is the earth re-made. But through the pot the earth re-made also re-appears. In short the clay pot, as an illustration of the original sense of this work of fictionalizing, *re-members* (transforms and preserves) the given earth. Re-membering as a work of fictionalizing *preserves* what is already given or made by *transforming* it.

Martin Heidegger (1971) has described the origin of the work of art in much the same way in which this work of fictionalizing has been described, and I make mention of this point here because it allows me to emphasize once again that the work of re-membering belongs to the creative process. In re-membering the past the patient in psychotherapy is engaged in the process of re-shaping the given of his or her life into a vessel which contains it. And that vessel, the clay pot which the patient makes, is nothing less than the story which is told, a story which preserves the past by re-shaping it. The containing and holding aspects of story are given, moreover, in its etymology for it is related to the Greek *eidos* which means the idea, form, or shape of things. In addition, story is kin to the words wise and wisdom as well as to the term guise which means the manner or appearance of things, their disguise which originally means the way in which something reveals and conceals or preserves itself. Finally, story means in its most immediate sense simply to see, to guide, or to show the way. The story through which the patient re-members (transforms and preserves) the past is, then, a way of seeing, a guide, something which shows the way of his or her life. It is the manner, guise, or appearance of things, the way in which the things and events of one's life are revealed and preserved. It is the form or shape of these things of one's life, the way in which they are held and contained. And as such and in all these ways the story through which the patient re-members his or her life, the story which is the creation of psychotherapy as a creative process, is a kind of wisdom. It is a psychological wisdom which is nothing less than the power to hear within the facts of a life the speaking of a tale.

CONCLUSION

The past which any individual *knows* about his or her life is essentially different from a past in which one can *believe*. A past which lies between the boundaries of knowledge and ignorance is a matter of mind. Belief, however, belongs to the realm of the human heart (Romanyshyn, 1982) and it is to this domain that a past which lies between the boundaries of belief and doubt belongs. Psychotherapy as a creative process becomes, therefore, a matter of awakening the believing heart and specifically of awakening those dimensions of human experience, courage, and memory, which the history of words tell us belong to the human heart. To re-member one's past takes courage, that kind of courage May (1975) has described in relation to the creative process. It is the courage to dare to make out of the otherwise mundane facts of one's life a believable story, a tale by which to live. And such courage is, I believe, in the final analysis akin to the act of love. Re-membering the past of one's life, then, is a work of Eros, a work which not only knits together the scattered fragments of a hitherto unreflective life, but also and perhaps more profoundly takes up a heritage as a destiny. It is what the philosopher Nietzsche described as *amor fati*, the love of one's fate in the sense of embracing it as a work to be done.

The symptom and the dream are, I believe, the most important elements in this work, for in the symptom lingers something of one's fate denied, and in the dream there is whispered something of the work to be done. Or perhaps in a more dramatic sense it is better to say that in the symptom resides the figure waiting to tell its tale, while in the dream there is something of the story which cannot yet be spoken in words. To conclude this essay, I want to end with a dream brought to me by a woman in her mid-30s who was troubled at the time with vague anxieties, a gnawing sense of restlessness, and a growing fear that she was wasting her life in meaningless tasks. In addition, within the previous five years this woman had had two major surgeries, one of which involved her knee and the other her jaw. At the time of her dream she was in a pottery class, experiencing the frustration of being unable to shape a pot which would hold together.

> I was in the studio, trying to make a pot, but it kept breaking. Finally in frustration I gave up and went outside to lie down. I fell asleep and in my dream I was approached by a very tiny man who was shaped like a clay pot. The pot itself was his body and his face was very clearly presented. At first I was frightened but my fascination got the better of me. As the pot-man approached he said in a voice that sounded very old, "Hold and shape it gently." Then I woke up and went back to the studio.

Knees and jaws are bones and joints. As bones they are a very basic given of one's life, the rock-hard but also fragile stuff out of which one is made and is kin to the earth. As joints, however, they are a flexible medium, the means by which one extends oneself in gesture and in speech into the world. Caught between the inflexible rigidity of bone and the call to move out and to speak, this woman was unable either to hold on and settle into her bones or to use them flexibly to fashion a world for herself. At the moment she would begin to shape a life — the clay pot in the dream, the given stuff of the earth — she would press too hard, tighten up, become stiff and rigid. As a consequence, her efforts, she said, would always end in failure and in fear of beginning again. But in the dream she was addressed as she was told in a masculine voice to take hold of things more gently. And here, I believe, in this voice the symptoms which had resided in her bones as rigidity and inflexibility became a form, a figure. Through a dream she was told and we might say even given permission to take told of things more lightly and playfully. A passion for form, which May (1975) again ties so closely to the creative process, spoke to her and in the guise of a dream figure which voiced her other masculine side. Form and shape your life, the figure said, but in such a way which listens to what is given.

We talked very briefly about the dream, acknowledging primarily that it seemed to be asking of her to recognize that she was being addressed. If she was going to create, then what *she* would form would have to preserve (respect and care for) what was given. Shortly thereafter she made her first pot and followed it with a series of what she warmly called her "uglies."

I know of no other kind of patient in psychotherapy than the one who is faced with this challenge to create, with this task to remember one's life as story. The symptom is a failed work, or perhaps it is better to say a work which remains unfinished; and neurotic suffering the obverse of creative struggling. What psychotherapy as a creative process offers, then, is the chance to discover the story that founds one's life as a heritage in order to take up the responsibility to continue its creation as one's destiny.

REFERENCES

Capra, F. (1982). *The turning point*. New York: Simon & Schuster.

Coleridge, S.T. (1968). *Biographia literaria*. in M.H. Abrams (Gen. Ed.), *The Norton anthology of English literature* (pp. 261-282). New York: W.W. Norton.

Eliot, T.S. (1971). Little Gidding. In *Four quartets*. New York: Harcourt, Brace & World.

Guggenbuhl-Craig, A. (1976). *Power and the helping professions*. Dallas: Spring Publications.

Heidegger, M. (1971). The origin of the work of art. In A. Hofstadter (Trans.), *Poetry, language, thought* (pp. 15-87). New York: Harper and Row.

Maria, J. (1970). *Jose Ortega y Gasset: Circumstance and vocation* (F.M. Lopez-Morillas, Trans.). Norman, OK: University of Oklahoma Press.

May, R. (1975). *The courage to create*. New York: W.W. Norton.

Merleau-Ponty, M. (1962). *Phenomenology of perception* (C. Smith, Trans.). New York: The Humanities Press.

Minkowski, E. (1970). *Lived time* (N. Metzel, Trans.). Evanston, IL: Northwestern University Press.

Rank, O. (1959). *The myth of the birth of the hero* (P. Freund, Ed.). New York: Vintage Books.

Ricoeur, P. (1978). The question of proof in Freud's writings. In C.E. Reagan and D. Stewart (Eds.), *The philosophy of Paul Ricoeur* (pp. 184-210). Boston: Beacon Press.

Rifkin, J. (1984). *Algeny*. New York: Penguin Books.

Romanyshyn, R. (1982). *Psychological life: From science to metaphor*. Austin, TX: University of Texas Press.

Romanyshyn, R. (1986). Mirror as metaphor of psychological life. In K.M. Yardley and T.M. Honess (Eds.), *Self and identity: Psychosocial perspectives* (pp. 297-305). New York: John Wiley.

Van den Berg, J.H. (1972). *A different existence*. Pittsburgh, PA: Duquesne University Press.

Discovery in Psychotherapy:
The Role of the Creative Patient

Anne E. Foon

SUMMARY. The conditions for patient creativity in psychotherapy are considered. The most fundamental condition for creativity is considered to be the internal source or locus of individual control in the psychotherapeutic context. It is considered desirable that patients be encouraged to develop and maintain internal control orientations. Statements in therapy which tend to put the patient at the mercy of outside forces are considered to be inappropriate since they lead individuals away from the creative process of psychotherapy. These conceptual issues are explored with a view to strengthening the therapist's theoretical basis for successful therapeutic intervention.

Creativity underlies human life and yet this concept has rarely been systematically treated in the psychotherapy literature. This is perhaps not surprising given the innumerable sources of difficulty in appraising the effectiveness of psychotherapy in general, let alone the components of creativity in particular. The general conclusion from the literature seems to be that many behaviors that appear to change as a result of psychotherapy are actually influenced little or not at all by the therapy and that the observed changes are produced by endogenous processes of a counteractive sort (Garfield, 1978; Parloff, Waskow, & Wolpe, 1978). This is not to say, however, that psychotherapy is without merit. Psychotherapy can be helpful in a variety of direct and indirect ways by freeing the individual to think of new undertakings and to implement them. Needless to say, psychotherapy is no panacea insofar as creativity is

Dr. Anne E. Foon holds degrees in sociology and social/clinical psychology. She has held both research and teaching positions in community health and educational studies and presently teaches sociology and administration. Mailing address: Department of Psychology, Australian National University, GPO Box 4, Canberra, ACT 2601, Australia.

concerned. Nonetheless, the role of creativity in the self-discovery of patients in psychotherapy is an area of concern. This paper considers the conditions conducive to constructive creativity in psychotherapy. It is argued that the crucial condition for patient creativity is an internal source of control. Discovery in psychotherapy will, it is claimed, be facilitated by the establishment and maintenance of internal orientations.

Psychotherapy is a term used by many different people to refer to various realities. For the purposes of this paper, psychotherapy will denote that process involving a sufferer and a trained healer who engage in a series of fairly structured contacts which seek to produce certain changes in the sufferer's emotional state, attitudes, or behavior — changes that are desired by both sufferer and healer (adapted from Frank, 1961). As such, psychotherapy is used in its widest sense as help-giving of any kind.

The concept of creativity has also been variously defined. In this paper creativity will be considered in terms of self-actualization. The tendency toward self-actualization motivates both individual development and creative activities and achievement. In the words of Carl Rogers (1970), the creative process refers to "the emergence in action of a novel relational product, growing out of the uniqueness of the individual on the one hand and the materials, events, people or circumstances of his life on the other" (p. 139). He and others have gone on to delineate the elements that comprise the creative act as it occurs in psychotherapy.

The literature provides some evidence that focusing ability may increase during psychotherapy and lead to expressions of creativity. Also, research evidence has dealt with the effect of psychotherapy on productivity, a concept closely related to creativity (Stein, 1974).

Gendlin, Beebe, Cassens, Klein, and Oberlander (1968) have defined focusing ability as that capacity to focus directly on cognitive understanding and to carry it forward concretely with attention, with words, and with actions. These authors believe there is something similar going on in the creative process as that which occurs in focusing ability. For them, the creative individual turns his or her attention from the interpretation of well-articulated forms to those which are as yet unformulated. The creative person, they say, attends to conceptually vague impressions first and from these develop meaningful statements. Though they do not argue the case for psychotherapy, it would seem that if the aim of therapy is to enable the patient to carve out a personally meaningful life-space, the ability to interpret unformulated concepts and to make sense of them would seem to be an essential part of the psychotherapy process.

Gendlin et al. (1968) therefore claim a relationship between the ability to focus on vague preverbalized experiences and what goes on in the creative process. The evidence for such an association between focusing ability and creativity is tenuous, as these same authors demonstrate. In their study, they report associations between focusing ability and personality data for high school students. Among the personality characteristics found to correlate positively with focusing ability were intelligence, self-discipline, interpersonal skill, and compulsiveness. While some of these might be regarded as positively related to creativity (e.g., self-discipline), others are not (e.g., compulsiveness).

Productivity has been considered in the literature on creativity because of the possible links between the two concepts. For example, Wispe and Parloff (1965) compared the publication productivity of 55 male psychologists who had 60 or more hours of psychotherapy with a matched group of 55 psychologists who had neither considered nor received therapy. These authors found that while objective measures did not support the idea that psychotherapy has a positive effect, those based on subjective evaluations did. In other words, while on the one hand, they found an association between subjective evaluations of satisfaction with psychotherapy and subjective measures of productivity, on the other hand, no significant association was reported between satisfaction with therapy and objective measures of productivity.

This kind of discrepancy in results no doubt reflects the diverse range of outcomes which can be considered relevant in discussions of psychotherapy. In particular, these differences have been noted as being identical to the differences in deliberations that frequently emerge between creative people who have undergone psychotherapy and other persons (Stein, 1974, p. 80). Clearly, as Wispe and Parloff point out, "having had therapy" is not a unitary variable.

One of the major problems in discussing the components of creativity is that, at present, relatively little is known about the value and effectiveness of different approaches to stimulating creativity. While the majority of work has been conducted on personality factors that are linked to creativity, there is no consistent evidence on the kind of person who is likely to be creative in therapy (Fried, 1964; Gilchrist, 1972; Maslow, 1972).

There is a clear need for a more general conceptualization of the discovery of patient creativity in psychotherapy. We need to look to the ephemeral and the subjective in psychotherapy more than to individual's traits that are consistent and objectifiable if we are to appraise psychotherapy's value for the establishment of creativity. While recognizing that viewing psychotherapy as subjective reality may put it beyond the kinds of criticism that objective research can typically support, this need not be the case. Attempting to be objective in relation to an activity that is subjective is a dilemma which must be recognized. However, it need not put tests of conceptualizations beyond reach.

The occupational hazard in psychotherapy appears to be the concentration on "objective" psychopathology. It should be possible for psychotherapists to concentrate on the subjective qualities of individuals. Too often, however, there is minimal emphasis on these traits (Branch, 1966). The implication of focusing on symptoms without regard to the subjective reality accompanying them is to view creativity as a symptom like any other symptom. If patients' creativity is treated as a neurotic symptom that stands in the way of their more complete growth and maturity, then they may be faced with the choice of whether they want to continue with the symptom or dissolve or diminish it by diverting energy from it to other purposes. If the latter decision is made, then creativity may be diminished.

Clearly this sort of argument is in conflict with the notion that creativity is a necessary resource for the patient's struggle back to mental health (Branch, 1966; Torrance, 1970; Weigert, 1965). If we are to take seriously the notion that the subjective orientation of patients is fundamental to the development of the creative potential essential for success in psychotherapy, then we need to assess the major preconditions for the establishment of creativity in psychotherapy. The remainder of this paper will focus on the major factor that appears to precede creativity and the therapist's role in the establishment and maintenance of this condition. The construct referred to is the patient's possession of an internal control orientation and the ability of therapists to avoid external explanations for symptoms.

It is not a new idea that the most fundamental condition of creativity is that the source or locus of evaluative judgment is internal (Rogers, 1951, 1970). The value of the product is, for the creative patient, established not by the praise or criticism of others, but by oneself. This orientation does not imply that a person is oblivious to, or unwiling to be aware of, the judgments of others. It is simply that the basis of evaluation lies within oneself, in one's own reaction to and appraisal of one's product. If, to the person, it has the feel of being an actualization of potentialities in oneself, which beforehand had not existed and are now emerging into existence, then it is satisfying and creative and no outside evaluation can change that fundamental fact. This sort of argument is in line with the work reported earlier (Gendlin et al., 1968; Wispe & Parloff, 1965). Again it would seem that evaluating the subjective components of individuals' evaluation of psychotherapy is crucial to any investigation of the creative potential of psychotherapy.

The very nature of the internal conditions of creativity, described above, imply that they cannot be forced, but must be permitted to emerge. The important question becomes, then, how can therapists etablish the external conditions which will foster and nourish these internal conditions? Essentially the major condition for fostering creativity in psychotherapy is the provision of a clinical environment in which external evaluation is absent (Barron, 1969; Rogers, 1970; Taylor, 1972).

If judgments based on external standards are not being made by the therapist, then patients can be much more open to their own experiences, can recognize their own likes/dislikes and so on. This leads to the possibility that when patients recognize that the locus of their evaluation is within themselves, they move toward creativity. If this is the case patients need to be encouraged to establish and to maintain internal orientations. When patients are told they must be concerned with what others think, they are being led away from creativity. When therapists cease to form judgments of the patient from their own locus of evaluation, they are fostering creativity (Rogers, 1970).

The fearful therapist may try to control the behavior and attitudes of people he or she is responsible for. Control restricts the range of behaviors of those controlled, encourages conformity rather than creativity, and tends to produce dependent behavior. Therapists release creativity by trusting, open, allowing, and interdependent actions. The high-creativity therapist is likely to allow for more self-determination and self-assessment of progress toward patient goals than the low-creativity therapist.

The growth of creativity is probably cumulative in some way. Independent patients create their own goals: they seek new experiences, risk new behaviors, test limits, explore boundaries, and so on. The more the therapist creates conditions in which patients can initiate, feel responsible for the process and feel free to create their own goals, the more the therapist creates the external conditions that maximize the possibility of the establishment and growth of the patient's creative potential. Therapists who appear impositional and controlling are likely to impede creativity within psychotherapy. Therapists who wish to optimize creativity must avoid statements that tend to put the patient at the mercy of external forces and instead focus on the elimination or reduction of restraining forces (Taylor, 1972).

The nondirective technique, broadly applied, is an excellent example of the use of this principle in psychotherapy. It has the advantage of keeping the therapist's remarks at the same level as the patient's, at least in terms of manifest content. The principle that therapists should let their patients be what they want to be in psychotherapy seems nonsense on the surface. After all, isn't it the aim of psychotherapy to induce changes in the behavior of the patient (Barron, 1963)? While clearly the removal of symptoms and the inducement of positive changes are generally desirable in therapy, the argument here is that above all else it is important that patients freely choose what they want. If the therapist accepts this principle, and does not impose his or her own set of evaluative criteria, then he or she is assisting the creative process (Barron, 1969). Also in this way therapists can maximize their role in guiding patients toward constructive change.

It is not the wish of the author to give the impression that individuals should become totally self-centered with the consequence of becoming personally and socially disruptive. Clearly, creative activity, like any other, must be fostered within boundaries. Freedom in psychotherapy does not imply the acceptance of deviant acts but rather it is concerned with permitting individuals to have complete freedom of symbolic expression (Deri, 1984; Wenkart, 1965). The argument here is that patients must be able to develop and to maintain orientations that allow them to make statements in an open way. Therapists need to become aware of what they are saying to patients with regard to causality because this will most probably affect the nature of creative expression.

Freedom to express the self also implies responsibility. The type of freedom from external evaluation, described above, results from responsibility to oneself which fosters the development of a secure locus of evaluation within oneself and therefore tends to bring about the inner conditions of constructive creativity.

Without wanting to simplify the obviously complex nature of the creative process in psychotherapy, it seems that there is a certain similarity between the notions put forward above and the concept of locus of control promulgated by Rotter (1966). The need for the patient to possess an internal locus of evaluation for events and to accept responsibility for those same events in order to facilitate the development of creativity may be understood in terms of the broader development of the individual's cognitive orientations. Rotter's ideas of control orientation were based on the potential value of particular cognitive sets for positive personal and social outcomes. In the clinical context, he applied the locus of control construct to an important question: namely, why some clients appear to gain from new experiences or to change their behavior as a result of new experiences, while others seem to discount new experiences by attributing them to chance or to other people and not to their own behavior or characteristics.

In the psychotherapeutic literature there is some focus on individual responsibility; internal control orientations are more facilitative of favorable therapeutic outcomes than external control orientations, whose focus is on external causality (Balch & Ross, 1975; Dowds, Fontana, Russakoff, & Harris, 1977; Manno & Marston, 1972; McGovern & Caputo, 1983). Clearly the relationship between locus of control and therapy outcome is not a direct one. A number of writers have investigated the importance of type of therapy for this relationship. Generally they have found that internals do better in nondirective therapies, whereas external clients perform better in directive therapies (Friedman & Dies, 1974; Kilmann & Howell, 1974; Kilmann & Sotile, 1976; Snowden, 1978).

It is true that these studies do not allow for comments to be made about associations between patient's locus of evaluation and creativity. Moreover, the results of such research efforts are confounded by poor sampling frames, lack of comparability in outcome measures, and the failure to follow up. Even so this research field does appear to hold some promise in providing guidelines for investigating the relationship between creativity and the important precondition of creativity, namely, internal evaluation of life events.

The reason for raising the possibility that internal control orientations and a concomitant avoidance of external explanations may be of importance for understanding the development of creativity in psychotherapy is not simply to provide a conceptual model for understanding the relationship, but to propose a number of hypotheses which are in principle testable and which could prove to be of some practical relevance. The hypotheses developed are as follows:

1. The more a patient is able to evaluate events from an internal perspective, the greater his or her creative potential.
2. The greater the creative potential of the patient, the greater the likelihood that he or she will benefit from therapies in which judgments based on external standards are not being made.
3. The extent to which different therapies provide freedom and responsibility will determine the degree of creativity among client groups, with analytically oriented therapies producing greater creativity in client groups than behavior therapies.

In this paper an attempt has been made to present a way of thinking about the creative' process in psychotherapy which could be open to objective test. It was pointed out that even though the association between creativity and psychological health is a crucial one, little attempt has been made to develop relationships between studies in the field of psychotherapy on the one hand and of creativeness on the other. It was considered desirable that the creative process in psychotherapy be taken as an essentially subjective experience, despite the obvious difficulties with such a position. It was argued that concepts like focusing ability and productivity were not very useful for exploring the creative potentialities of patients in therapy, nor were personality variables in general.

Instead, a position was developed, based on a number of previous conceptualizations, which claimed that the crucial precondition for creativity in therapy is that the patient's source or locus of evaluative judgment is internal. Hand in hand with this notion was the related concept that therapeutic settings were conducive to creativity insofar as external evaluations were absent. The therapist's potential role in establishing and maintaining the conditions under which patient's creative discovery could be achieved was considered at length. Finally, a number of hypotheses were developed employing Rotter's locus-of-control construct as a possible variable of importance for the development of patient creativity. While clearly the ideas presented are at a rudimentary stage, it is hoped that they might provide the basis for future investigations. It is an obvious though often neglected fact that individuals contain creative potential which helps them achieve flexible, efficient adjustments to life. It is the ability of therapists to utilize this potential in psychotherapy that poses an exciting challenge.

REFERENCES

Balch, P., & Ross, A.W. (1975). Predicting success in weight-reduction as a function of locus of control: A unidimensional and multi-dimensional approach. *Journal of Consulting and Clinical Psychology, 43*, 119.

Barron, F. (1963). *Creativity and psychological health*. New York: D. Van Nostrand.

Barron, F. (1969). *Creative person and creative process.* New York: Holt, Rinehart & Winston.

Branch, C.H.H. (1966). The therapist and human potentialities. In H.A. Otto (Ed.), *Explorations in human potentialities* (pp. 277-285). Illinois: Charles C Thomas.

Deri, S.K. (1984). *Symbolization and creativity*. New York: International Universities Press.

Dowds, B.N., Fontana, A.F., Russakoff, L.M., & Harris, M. (1977). Cognitive mediators between patients' social class and therapists' evaluations. *Archives of General Psychiatry, 34*, 917-920.

Frank, J. (1961). *Persuasion and healing: A comparative study of psychotherapy.* Baltimore: John Hopkins.

Fried, E. (1964). *Artistic productivity and mental health*. Illinois: Charles C Thomas.

Friedman, M.L., & Dies, R.R. (1974). Reactions in internal and external test-anxious students in counseling and behavior therapies. *Journal of Consulting and Clinical Psychology, 42*, 921.

Garfield, S.L. (1978). Research on client variables in psychotherapy. In S.L. Garfield & A.E. Bergin (Eds.), *Handbook of psychotherapy and behavior change: An empirical analysis* (2nd ed.) (pp. 191-232). New York: Wiley.

Gendlin, E.T., Beebe, J. III, Cassens, J., Klein, M., & Oberlander, M. (1968). Focusing ability in psychotherapy, personality and creativity. In J.M. Shlien (Ed.), *Research in psychotherapy, Vol. 3* (pp. 217-241). Washington, DC: American Psychological Association.

Gilchrist, M. (1972). *The psychology of creativity*. Melbourne: Melbourne University Press.

Kilmann, P.R., & Howell, P.J. (1974). The relationship between structure of marathon group therapy, locus of control, and outcome. *Journal of Consulting and Clinical Psychology, 42*, 912.

Kilmann, P.R., & Sotile, W.M. (1976). The effects of structured and unstructured leader roles on internal and external group participants. *Journal of Clinical Psychology, 32*, 846-863.

Manno, B., & Marston, A.R. (1972). Weight reduction as a function of negative covert reinforcement (sensitization) versus positive covert reinforcement. *Behavior Research and Therapy, 10*, 201-207.

Maslow, A.H. (1972). A holistic approach to creativity. In C.W. Taylor (Ed.), *Climate for creativity* (pp. 287-293). New York: Pergamon Press.

McGovern, M.P., & Caputo, G.C. (1983). Outcome prediction of inpatient alcohol detoxification. *Addictive Behaviors, 8*, 167-171.

Parloff, M.B., Waskow, I.E., & Wolpe, B.E. (1978). Research on therapist variables in relation to process and outcome. In S.L. Garfield & A.E. Bergin (Eds.), *Handbook of psychotherapy and behavior change: An empirical analysis* (2nd ed.). New York: Wiley.

Rogers, C.R. (1951). *Client-centered therapy: Its current practice, implications, and theory.* Boston: Houghton Mifflin.

Rogers, C.R. (1970). Towards a theory of creativity. In E. Vernon (Ed.), *Creativity: Selected readings* (pp. 137-154). Victoria: Penguin.

Rotter, J.B. (1966). Generalized expectancies for internal versus external control of reinforcement. *Psychological Monographs, 80*, (1 Whole No. 609).

Snowden, L.R. (1978). Personality tailored covert sensitization of heroin abuse. *Addictive Behavior, 3*, 43-49.

Stein, M.E. (1974). *Stimulating creativity, Vol. 1.* New York: Academic Press.

Taylor, C.W. (1972). Can organizations be creative too? On the importance of creativity. In C.W. Taylor (Ed.), *Climate for creativity* (pp. 1-22). New York: Pergamon Press.

Torrance, E.P. (1970). Causes for concern. In E. Vernon (Ed.), *Creativity: Selected readings.* Victoria: Penguin.

Weigert, E. (1965). The goal of creativity in psychotherapy. In H.M. Ruitenbeek (Ed.), *The creative imagination: Psychoanalysis and the genius of inspiration* (pp. 293-311). Chicago: Quadrangle Books.

Wenkart, A. (1965). Creativity and freedom. In H.M. Ruitenbeek (Ed.), *The creative imagination: Psychoanalysis and the genius of inspiration* (pp. 337-350). Chicago: Quadrangle Books.

Wispe, L.G., & Parloff, M.B. (1965). Impact of psychotherapy on the productivity of psychologists. *Journal of Abnormal Psychology, 700*, 188-193.

Creative Patient/Patient Therapist

Erling Eng

SUMMARY. The creative contribution to the psychotherapeutic situation is more likely to be attributed to the authorial (and authoritative!) therapist than to the patient. This obscures the extent to which the therapist is created by the patient in the service of his or her needs. It is only when the therapeutic situation as such is understood as creative for both participants that the creative role of the patient can be appreciated. The party played by the creativity of a patient is illustrated in a therapeutic incident with a traumatized Vietnam veteran.

The painted portrait is not precisely the production of the reflection and the image, as happens with waters, mirrors and shadows.

Plotinus, Enneads, VI.
4.10.11-13

The partnership of creative patient/patient therapist may be likened to that of reader/writer. Just as the writer is created by the reader through poem or book as the work of both, so the patient therapist is originally evoked by the creative patient. Here "evoked" also means "seen as." To be sure, the "creative patient" can be understood to refer to a certain kind of patient. Or, better, it can be understood as making this point: that over against the customary but unvoiced emphasis on the initiative of the therapist, the neglected initiative of the patient also calls for recognition.

Erling Eng, PhD, is a clinical psychologist at the V.A. Medical Center. He is also Clinical Professor, Department of Psychiatry, University of Kentucky. He has published in psychoanalytic, phenomenological, and history of science journals. Mailing address: V.A. Medical Center, Lexington, KY 40511.
This article is dedicated to the remaining unknown soldiers.

The patient therapist, suffering himself or herself to be open, suffering through its consequences — discovers how to become the therapist the patient needs to create. The sufferer, "patient," creates, that is, etymologically "makes grow," the therapist as one whom he or she needs to "suffer" in the sense of allowing himself or herself to be open — like, and yet unlike — the therapist.

The correspondence already is present at the outset of, indeed in our presence to/for one another. But it is somehow flawed, and it is this flawedness, *felure*, initially disclaimed by patients, which can come to be experienced by them as a requirement for discovery of meaning as they become creative. The experience of the correspondence may be more or less, even though it is always necessarily both. Less, I am also a sufferer as therapist, too; more, my presence as therapist is healing. That is, facilitating "wholeness." The correspondence as sameness in difference grows out of an earlier experience of difference in sameness between the partners, difference suffered as inseparable from a dissonance, gap, fracture, split within the patient and to a lesser degree in and by the therapist as well. It is through the experience of the variations in the quality and extent of our differences that the course of our relationship together is differentiated, and becomes in-formed.

In my work with a traumatized veteran, I often find that his hidden difference with a slain enemy is most deeply sought. He seeks him in his nightmares, to be made whole by his otherwise missing presence, whose absence he effected, and which had first validated him as a real soldier, no matter what his previous training. Years later, he now seeks that Other, vis-à-vis whom he was unconsciously confirmed as a soldier. He needs to find him to realize more fully what happened at that time, a profound transformation but lacking ritual enactment, and therefore remaining as a foreign body, a hidden body which he (and others) now dread. His creative effort, apparently spent in a senseless repetition of fragmented memories, continues to be frustrated until he is able to recover through the presence of the patient therapist that counterpart whose death discovered to him what it means to *be* a soldier, which as *being* can never be merely told to another, but only silently acknowledged among peers, for example what it means to be ready to die in carrying out what one believes to the will of one's people or country.

I recall a combat veteran, thrice subjected to extreme stress: tortured as a prisoner of war in Vietnam, victim of a land mine in

Korea, and finally manhandled by male hospital attendants after being misdiagnosed as paranoid schizophrenic. This man had survived to the extent of being able to partake of psychotherapy only because of his original basic strengths. One day, after we had been working together five days a week for up to an hour over a period of three or four weeks, he said, "I am having a flashback." I said to him, "Just go right ahead and tell me everything that's happening." He said, "I am firing at a VC (Viet Cong) and he is coming apart. I keep firing and he keeps coming apart." Puzzlement crept into his words. "I keep firing and firing and he doesn't fall. I can't understand it. Then I sit down and start crying." I said to him, "That VC was me. I am not afraid of you and so you couldn't kill me. When you realized this you sat down and began to cry. You realized that you were trying to kill the one you want to help you." He immediately said, "yes." Two days later he told me, "I've admitted to you that I haven't been able to fully trust you. But last night I had a dream, in which you were on my team (combat) in Vietnam." Not long after, the patient was discharged from the hospital, and I have not seen him again.

Whatever the now unanswerable questions about what happened then and there and about the further course of this man's life, I believe that just as a single decisive event comes to stand for the awe-filled realization of what it means to be a soldier, with the *possibility* of its *later* being experienced as a *trauma*, so too a single decisive event can come to stand for what it means to be, despite what one has done, a compassionate human being. The meaning of "patient" as one who suffers pain is now enhanced by the discovery of suffering as allowing, *acknowledging*, in which the opening of assent exceeds the closure of guilt. Only now can the sufferer suffer his suffering to be, without being tempted to demolish whatever it is by which he feels he has been betrayed, or without being tempted to demolish himself.

The patient therapist "suffers" the patient's painful suffering until the patient has replaced his mode of suffering with that complementary mode, the "allowance" of the therapist. I believe it was only when the veteran came to suffer from his unconscious attempt to inflict his suffering on myself as therapist that he was able to take his suffering more fully upon himself; this assumption of previously unacknowledged responsibility included an implicit realization and acceptance of the possible depth and range of human change. This creative patient was a team leader in Vietnam, and wherever he is now, I am sure I remain a part of his team. Admittedly, there is room at this point for discussion and conjecture about idealization and ambivalences. But there are also small victories which remain lasting because preserved as exemplary instances.

Such a "moment of truth" can remain as the counterpart and complement of that prior moment, whose inaccomplishment is experienced as a wound, retroflectively discovered as having been a "trauma." The realization of such a disclosure is often described by patients as more painful than what is remembered of that event, whose realization initially seems to be that of a repetition. But that the repetition should be even more trying than the original event does not comport with the view of repetition as an attempt to weaken the impact of the original experience. Coping involves more than that. Rather it suggests that only now is the full human significance of the earlier happening coming to be realized.

When patients describe the peculiar anguish of this post-experienced amplification of humanly incomplete events, I am reminded of the anguish which, sooner or later, and however displaced, seems to be inseparable from human change, with its challenge to the continuing creation of identity. (We are told that Joseph Conrad would beat on the door of his room after he had ordered his wife to lock him in, and not to let him out before he had completed his daily writing stint.)

What was originally a shattering discovery, a mere happening, grossly physical, is now completed, fulfilled in and through a deliberate activity, subtly physical as *voice* (logos) as accomplishment of meaning. There is a trauma of leaving and of loss, traumatic only in that it has not suffered the matching trauma of return, a life of betrayal and violence in the interval between the departure and the experience of return. Now the barrier of guilt also needs to be understood as the still intact ability to love, over against all of the evidence of one's violence in the painful interval.

The creativity of the patient I have told you about reminds me of the trials of Odysseus on his way home from the Trojan war. The Odyssey could not have been sung without the war, its prelude of traumatic losses related in the Iliad. The story of the Odyssey makes of its traditionally blind poet a seer, the creative counterpart of Oedipus. The seer is re-represented in the epic itself by the wily Odysseus, over against the vainglorious warrior Ajax, a second Oedipus, self-condemned, and blinded to the possibility of compassion in his pride and guilt.

Some Difficulties in Sustaining
a Therapeutic Presence
to the Creative Patient

William F. Fischer
Donald R. Hands

SUMMARY. Modes of successful therapeutic presence are not constant and invariable. Therapists are always vulnerable to being rendered anxious as well as to becoming caught up in other personal issues that can interfere with their professional work-attitudes. This vulnerability is explored in the specific case of patients who are perceived as unusually creative. Using an actual as well as a noted fictional situation, *Equus*, the authors distinguish between *admiration*, a presence that is seen as therapeutic, and *fascination*, a nontherapeutic and potentially destructive mode of being with the patient.

The character of the therapy relationship, especially the ways in which therapists are present to their patients, is a significant issue for most, if not all, systems of therapy. Beginning with Freud (1963) and his papers on technique, therapists have reflected upon the efficacy of these varied modes of presence. More recently, there has been an effort (Parloff, Waskow & Wolfe, 1978; Rogers, 1967; Truax & Mitchell, 1971; Whitehorn & Betz, 1954) to determine systematically as well as empirically which modes of therapist presence are associated with successful treatment. If we combine the most commonly held therapist beliefs with the results of these studies, we may conclude that an effective therapeutic presence to one's patient is likely to entail the following:

William F. Fischer, PhD, is Professor, and Donald R. Hands, PhD, is Assistant Professor in the Psychology Department, Duquesne University, Pittsburgh, PA 15282.

1. Being genuinely interested in who one's patient is, how he or she is struggling to construct as well as to understand his or her existence as meaningful despite a chronically oppressive sense of vulnerability to being rendered anxious;
2. Being able to sustain an accepting as well as empathic, communicative relationship with one's patient, regardless of the thoughts, feelings, and fantasies that he or she lives through and describes;
3. Authentically believing that one can be of help to one's patient and being able to live out that belief without conflict;
4. Being able to maintain a neutral position vis à vis the specific terms of one's patient's diverse conflicts; and
5. Being able to avoid simplistic, either-or modes of thinking about one's patient's existence.

As most of us have come to realize, however, the actualization of these modes of therapeutic presence is not an achievement we accomplish once and for all. It varies from patient to patient, even from issue to issue or from session to session with the same patient. In other words, despite our respective personal analyses or experiences of some other form of therapy, we too are vulnerable, at least some of the time, to interfering, if not debilitating, anxiety. With patients whose attributes or styles evoke a profound sense of deficiency, we tend to adopt modes of presence that may also be self-centered and exploitative. That is to say, with these patients we implicitly, if not explicitly, attempt to gratify our own frustrated desires and/or resolve our own heretofore-unsurpassed conflicts.

The creative patient, whether artistic or intellectual, can call forth any number of these self-centered and exploitative modes from certain therapists. Consider the following examples: the first is an unabridged description of his experience of working with an obsessive, albeit creative theologian/clergyman given by an interested colleague; the second is a characterization of Dr. Dysart's struggles with his schizophrenic patient, Alan, as described by Peter Shaffer (1974) in his play, *Equus*.

A few years ago, I worked with a moderately obsessive, yet distinctly creative young clergyman. While we spent many hours exploring his oppressive yet abiding inclination to doubt the seriousness of his commitments to his congregation as well as to his God, we only intermittently discussed the specifics of his innovative approach to theology. Still, whenever he focused upon that aspect of his vocation, for example, the context of describing a seminar that he was leading, or while ridiculing certain members of a panel upon which he was serving, I would be distracted from my usually empathic presence to him. Suddenly, I would experience myself as excited, even fascinated, but also as vaguely unintegrated and needy. My own unresolved and to some extent unacknowledged conflicts concerning religious affiliation and practice would unexpectedly come to the fore and *I would feel that my patient might be able to help me,* that I wanted to hear him describe in detail his approach to theology. Occasionally, I felt the urge to ask him specific questions and would even fantasize what it might be like to attend one of his seminars. Of course, I realized that all of this was rather inappropriate, that I was no longer empathically present to him, and that as long as he was my patient I could not confound our relationship in these ways. Still, I didn't want to refer him elsewhere; I wanted to keep him as my patient and as a potential, if not actual, spiritual guide. Hence, I told myself that I could wait until the therapy was completed. Needless to say, this resolution was exceedingly difficult to keep. Every once in a while I would find myself trying to manipulate the direction and themes of our dialogue so that he would be more likely to speak of his theological beliefs. Finally, I admitted to myself that it would not work, that if I wanted to talk theology with him, I should do so, but only after I had referred him to another therapist. This I finally did.

Based upon a newspaper account of a teenager's mutilation of the eyes of six horses, *Equus* sensitively depicts Dr. Dysart's personal struggle to sustain a therapeutic presence to Alan Strang, an apparently schizophrenic 17-year-old. Flattered by the referring magistrate's characterization of him as "the boy's only hope," Dr. Dysart takes a sudden and inordinate interest in Alan, who quickly becomes the focus of his professional and personal life. It should be noted that prior to the referral, Dr. Dysart has been slowly realizing that his project to build an orderly, predictable, and routine world within the confines of his hospital practice and marriage is destroying him; his work as well as his marriage are lived perfunctorily and without passion; he is "burnt out" and "dried up." His name, Dysart, literally means "the one who has lost his art."

Instinctively, he turns to Alan as a plant turns to the sun. He lives the boy as having magnetic power over him and clearly regards him as a creative young man, despite the bizarre, savage quality of his actions. Fascinated with and envious of Alan's passion, his willingness to act upon his feelings, Dr. Dysart frequently abandons or is distracted from his more typical therapeutic modes of presence, for example, he talks to Alan about his own personal life, he becomes careless about scheduling sessions, he dreams about the boy and is disturbed by his reproaches. Finally, he engaged Alan in a power struggle over who is to be the therapist and who is to be the patient. In some sense he constitutes and lives Alan as the patient who holds out the possibility of healing him, the doctor.

It is around the issue of who represents mental health and hence, who is to become like whom, that the drama unfolds. Is Alan to become another Dysart-like man, uncommitted and without passion, mechanically moving through life in a perfunctory manner? Is he to defend himself against the power of Eros by avoidance, impotence, and overcontrol? Clearly, he is caught up in an exciting, yet dangerous, newly sexualized world. He has already tried to gratify his passions in the stable with the result that he was overcome by guilt and shame, and therefore found it necessary to mutilate the eyes of the onlooking horses.

In spite of his difficulties, Dr. Dysart manages to establish a working alliance with Alan. He acknowledges to himself the character of his unhealthy attraction to the boy and resolutely struggles to adhere to the standards of good practice. Ultimately, he succeeds in offering what we are led to believe is effective treatment, even though he himself searches for healing in the process. His final comments reflect his recognition of his ambiguous relations with Alan: "Passion you see, can be destroyed by a doctor. It cannot be created." In the end, Dr. Dysart respected his patient's otherness and resisted the temptation to recreate him in his own likeness; still less did he try to therapeutically denude him of his passion. Rather, he sought to assist the boy by helping him to redirect and rechannel his desires. At the same time, he struggled to rediscover and reappropriate his own.

In each of these examples, the therapist becomes fascinated with his patient, at least temporarily. The obsessive clergyman as well as the 17-year-old schizophrenic are each experienced as creatively embodying that which their respective therapists have lived, if not acknowledged, as lacking in their own lives. Confronted with such patients, both therapists thematically rediscover certain of their own as yet unaccepted limits and deficiencies. Although each struggles with the temptation to surreptitiously use his patient in an effort to ameliorate and/or to flee from those limits and deficiencies, both ultimately accept their respective modes of indigence and live out their commitments to their patients.

It seems to us that these examples bring into focus one of the principal problems that therapists face when working with creative patients. Despite the diverse forms of psychopathology that the latter typically embody, they can also evoke profound fascination. Their therapists, depending upon the extent to which they have come to terms with themselves, can be vulnerable to humiliating comparisons and to feelings of deficiency, whether these have been self- or patient-instigated. In such a state, it is not difficult for therapists to fall into defensive, self-centered, and exploitative modes of presence. Unlike admiration, where therapists genuinely respect and affirm the otherness of their patients, fascination is not a therapeutic mode of relating.

REFERENCES

Freud, S. (1963). *Therapy and technique: Essays on dream interpretation, hypnosis, transference, free association, and other techniques of psychoanalysis* (P. Rieff, Ed.). New York: Collier Books.

Parloff, M.B., Waskow, I.E., & Wolfe, B.E. (1978). Research on therapist variables in relation to process and outcome. In S.L. Garfield & A.E. Bergin (Eds.), *Handbook of psychotherapy and behavior change: An empirical analysis* (2nd ed., pp. 233-282). New York: Wiley.

Rogers, C.R. (Ed.). (1967). *The therapeutic relationship and its impact: A study of psychotherapy with schizophrenics*. Madison, WI: University of Wisconsin Press.

Schaffer, P. (1975). *Equus*. New York: Avon.

Truax, C.B., & Mitchell, K.M. (1971). Research on certain therapist interpersonal skills in relation to process and outcome. In A.E. Bergin & S.L. Garfield (Eds.), *Handbook of psychotherapy and behavior change: An empirical analysis* (pp. 169-203). New York: Wiley.

Whitehorn, J.C., & Betz, B.J. (1954). A study of psychotherapeutic relationships between physicians and schizophrenic patients. *American Journal of Psychiatry, 3*, 321-331.

To Cause to Come into Existence:
The Creative Patient

Francis J. Peirce

SUMMARY. Creativity represents the struggle to develop, affirm, and celebrate individuality. The creative patient can use creativity to contend with life, to distort it, or to escape from it. The therapeutic success of the therapist's work depends on the ability to recognize one's own being separate from the patient. Four patients are discussed.

Create . . . 1. to cause to come into existence; make; originate 2. to bring about; give rise to; cause.
Creator . . . 1. one who creates 2. (C−) God.

(Guralnik, 1979)

The patient in therapy is creative, one who creates, one who causes to come into existence. The creative act in psychotherapy is to create being, to exist. It is the act of will, determination by which the patient chooses to be. This is the process whereby patients affirm and claim their own being by recognizing responsibility and freedom for their separate, lonely, terrified, and meaningless selves.

The therapist is the creative helper who brings his or her own creation of being into a relationship with the patient in such ways that the patient is enabled and encouraged to "cause to exist." The unsuccessful therapist is the one who fails to recognize his or her own being separate from the patient's. The helping relationship becomes a confusing defeating symbiosis of two who are unable to contend with their apartness. As this happens the therapist assumes

---

Dr. Francis J. Peirce is Professor of Social Work at The University of Oklahoma in Norman. He is also a psychotherapist in private practice in Shawnee, OK. Mailing address: School of Social Work, The University of Oklahoma at Norman, 1005 Jenkins St., Rhyne Hall, Rm. 211, Norman, OK 73019.

responsibility for the patient's life and feels guilty and inadequate when improvement is not forthcoming. The creative act of helping is not the act of creating the other, but rather, having the courage to be in a posture that permits the patient to change.

This means that all of us are creative; we must create to exist. Each of us creates our own being, our own existence as we make our way through life. So, the creative person it not a special category of patient or therapist. In each case, creativity represents the struggle to develop, affirm, and celebrate individuality. The innovative and unique activities of many patients and therapists are simply tools used for the overarching struggle to create personal being. These may or may not serve the cause of personal existence.

Lou Ella, twenty-nine and single, is a "born again" Christian who came for therapy to deal with anxiety and guilt over being sexually molested as a child. The offender was an older male friend of the family. His activity was limited to stroking and fondling Lou Ella and to placing her hand on his genitals. He insured her silence and compliance by threats of physical harm to her and her pets and by threats of social ostracism. Lou Ella has lived with this secret all her life. Recently she read an article that reached her because of its emphasis on the secrecy and shame of victims of sexual abuse. She spoke with her pastor who referred her to the local mental health clinic, and she was in turn referred to me. I was not sure that I should treat her. We discussed this and other options. She decided to work with me rather than to be referred to a group of adult women molested as children. She said that telling her secret to her pastor and to me had freed her from some of the bonds of silence, but attending a group, even one with others with similar experiences, would compromise her secret too gravely.

As we explored her life, it became clear that Lou Ella lived a very constricted and colorless life. She is quite active in her church, participating several days and nights each week. She is a competent employee in a large business. She has only two or three friends and is close to no one. She has never dated the same man more than twice and tends to romanticize about a grade-school sweetheart and a young man in the church who is separated but not divorced from his wife. Inasmuch as she finds divorce unacceptable, he is unavailable. She lives in the same community with her parents and sees little of them. The only close and warm relationship she remembers in her life was with her Grandfather, and even in this relationship she often felt that she somehow failed him.

For Lou Ella, then, the act of seeking therapy was one of remarkable courage. The crucial issue in treatment was to capitalize on this effort and to help her expand the boundaries of her life. In this effort, we achieved some success but ultimately failed when her will and my skill faltered.

Lou Ella's major "extracurricular" interest is writing short stories. These tend to be somewhat idealized, poetic romances. She has had nothing published except in a magazine that prints for pay. Through this magazine she was invited to a national conference of an association of short-story authors. She was given one of several dozen awards for "creative literary work." It was apparent to me that the magazine and conference were a scam but a relatively harmless one. The trip to the conference was Lou Ella's first flight as well as the first time she stayed in a large hotel or traveled alone. She planned the trip and experienced it with much fear and anxiety. As we discussed it, we agreed that it would be "good for her." It may have been, I don't know. Shortly after the trip she terminated therapy by failing appointments and not reappointing. Our work had threatened her vows of silence and this in turn left her guilt ridden and terrified. The trip precipitated her ending because it was "good for her," and she didn't see herself as good enough.

It is clear, in retrospect, that Lou Ella's traumatic childhood experience was the dominant event in her life, and secrecy the dominant theme. She and I agreed that what had happened was not her "fault." It was clear that this agreement was cognitive and not affective. She also became increasingly uncomfortable with my knowledge of her secret and probably came to resent that I knew. In addition, I was not clear about the vital importance of her church work and her writing. These, with her job, provided a protective structure that enabled her to exist. Our mistake was that we both wanted her to "function more fully," "to be more alive," and to "find more meaning in her life." I failed to help her see the meaning that already existed and didn't see the crucial import for her to keep her secret. The rigid structure of her life was essential to her being. Our efforts to create a new level of being were too threatening. The trip to the conference highlighted this and precipitated her ending.

Lou Ella saw her short stories as original and sensitive. I saw them as primitive and juvenile but as "a useful tool to help her expand her consciousness." Both of us were wrong! In my pompous but unspoken condescension I failed to see that with her writing she created an inner life connected to others that had more color and vitality than the dull reality of her existence. Instead of pushing her to join the Sooner Prose and Poetry club, I might have read her work with her to explore its meaning to her. I didn't, and we both failed to see that in her stories she does "function more fully," and "experience more meaning."

The final issue in my work with Lou Ella had to do not only with my failure to respect her right to create herself as she wished but with my assumption of primary responsibility for change through therapy. Somehow, without realizing it, I came to act as if I were responsible for her change. This was a response to her childhood trauma and her paucity of adult resources. So I ignored the strengths and assets that she had, and became God, the creator, the sculptor of her life. She accepted this at first and then demonstrated her autonomy by leaving therapy. We can, each of us, be God the parent and creator for ourselves; however, we cannot be the Creator for others. When we, wittingly or unwittingly, try, our work is doomed to failure.

My work with Lou Ella foundered because of my conviction that she had limited creative potential. Terry suffers severe and exquisite anguish that is generated by an uncontrolled abundance of imagination. His creativity is limitless, as are its painful results. A noted philosopher and historian at a small university, Terry has the capacity to visualize and to logically make connections that the rest of us earth-bound plodders barely recognize until his trenchant analysis makes them abundantly clear. This exercise in intellectual creation is exciting, enlightening, and oftentimes embarrassing to the rest of us. Terry has, for example, connected faculty peer evaluations with leading the Jews to the gas chambers of the holocaust. He develops lucid philosophical and sociological explanations for oppression and poverty. There is little about humans' inhumanity to other humans that escapes his sensitive analysis. He is an outstanding and creative thinker. He is also largely incapacitated by black waves of depression. He sees every flaw in humanity and he incorporates these into his being, they become the core of his existence. His knowledge, his brilliant analysis of the human condition result in a profound disabling depression. He has quit working and lives a semireclusive life using a bitter and sardonic wit as his primary buffer against a world he perceives as violent, inhumane, and vulgar. He accepts that he does not have the "give," "bounce," or resilience that permit the rest of us to live in this ugly, sordid world.

He is puzzled when others console him by telling him that he "knows too much," or "cares too much." He has tried therapy. He found the therapist to be "stupid" (probably true), and was furious when he was "accused of introjection, projection, and annihilatory fantasies." Terry has created his existence, his being, in a world where no one can help him, much less understand his world. His therapist was not brilliant enough to recognize the reality of Terry's world nor patient enough to find a way into it so as to be there with Terry. In fairness, it must be recognized that Terry's world is hardly one that is easily entered. So he lives on there, largely isolated, unable to escape, and not sure he should if he could.

Creativity for some is a matter of survival. Some, like Terry, create their own prison; others are captives of society's prisons. To get out or even to function minimally, they invent ingenious Rube Goldberg contraptions that facilitate a kind of truce with society. Marlow is a six-year-old with multiple problems who is under the care of the state. He has a major speech handicap, and an "attention-deficit disorder," or a "pervasive development disorder," or both, depending on which consultant you listen to. He wets the bed, trashes his foster home, is physically aggressive with his foster parents, and disrupts the school with his behavior, especially his Superman game (ta ta ta-da – DUPERMAN). Two people – his biological mother and his foster mother – understand most of what he says. He loves them both deeply and would be happiest if he and his biological mother could live as foster children with his foster mother. Three people – his foster father, his teacher and a caseworker no longer working with him – understand much of what he says. Everyone else understands very little of his speech. With them, he responds as the rest of us do when not heard or understood, he speaks LOUDER AND SLOWER. When this doesn't work he shows his creative talent and communicates with wordless charades. He looks about and finds "sounds alike," "looks alike" and "colored alike." He writes and draws in the air and acts out more roles than Richard Pryor and Robin Williams combined. He engages in beautiful, animated, and creative communication. This is effective with those who respect his right to have his own symbol system. Most children find little that is strange about his communication efforts. His biggest problems come from the professionals who are supposed to understand him and to help him. Too many of them find him to be "an atypical autistic," "pre-operational," or "bizarre." The failure of teachers, psychologists, psychiatrist, and social workers to see the rich, innovative capacity of the boy is appalling. This rejection of his integrity, his right to be, means that he is lost, he will not be helped, and that he will bang about an inadequate public system of child care until he so offends us that he can be locked away out of sight. Wherever he is, he will hold on to at least a part of his being and maintain much of his creative, albeit puzzled and ambivalent connection with the world.

Jimmy Bob, on the other hand, is using his creativity processes to escape further and further into himself. Jimmy Bob was referred for therapy after discharge from an alcohol treatment program. He was described as sober and doing well on the ward, but also as stilted, aloof, and distant. He had worked as a restaurant manager and bartender in a motel in a small city in the oil patch. He had "used" alcohol and drugs as an adolescent and young adult. Neither had interfered with his life until he took the bartending job. Then he found that he needed alcohol in order to relate to others. As a result, he nearly lost his job and voluntarily entered treatment. Without alcohol or drugs he found that he could not contend with others. He became increasingly distant and was near a point of total separation from others. Prior to hospitalization he had found comfort and pleasure in writing poetry. His poems are about souls lost in space seeking a safe haven and peace through communion with a benign and loving power. His poems do not include other people, they were populated only by the plaintive prayerful voice of the author. They are essentially a prayer for release from the hell of other people. In therapy, Jimmy Bob became increasingly distant and made fewer efforts to connect with me or with others. He spent increasingly more time discussing his poetry and the fantasies attendant to those. He told me that he wanted to stay in contact with me and others even though his retreat into self was not frightening. However, the world of other people was too harsh, too unfair, and too painful. His withdrawal into poetic fantasy provided the peace and comfort he so desperately wanted. We explored options, including medication and rehospitalization, but he didn't want "legal drugs," couldn't afford private hospitalization, and was properly terrified of public institutions. The last I heard from him he called to say that he was moving. I assume that he has moved into the fantasy world he had created. This permitted him to avoid the demanding task of creating his being in a world he could not understand or manage.

The creative patient can use creativity to contend with life, to distort it, or to escape from it. Lou Ella found the responsibility to re-create her being too demanding and frightening, and chose to not change. Terry's creativity is so depressingly overwhelming that he can barely function. Jimmy Bob creates his own separate world rather than muster the courage to live in this one. Only Marlow continues to struggle to create his own being in an uncaring impersonal system. Of the four persons I have discussed, Marlow is the one who is taking on the world and struggling for his right to an existence of integrity and dignity. He is probably doomed to failure, to be crushed by an oppressive system that will not tolerate creative rebels.

REFERENCE

Guralnik, D. (1979). *Webster's new world dictionary*. New York: Popular Library.

On Keeping Out of the Briar Patch: A Family-Ecological Systems Approach to Treating the Behavior Problems of Creative Adolescents

Charles M. Borduin
Barton J. Mann

SUMMARY. During the past decade, multisystemic models of adolescent behavior disorders have received strong empirical support. In this article, the individual and systemic determinants of behavior problems in creative adolescents are described. It is shown that adolescent creativity is related to a variety of individual, familial, and extrafamilial variables, and that these variables shape the behaviors of creative adolescents. A multisystemic approach for the assessment and treatment of creative adolescents with behavior problems is also described. It is suggested that mental health professionals who treat the behavior problems of creative adolescents should consider the adolescent's family-ecological context when planning therapeutic interventions.

Adolescence has often been described as a highly turbulent period characterized by emotional instability; distortions of reality;

Charles M. Borduin, PhD, is Assistant Professor of Psychology at the University of Missouri-Columbia. His main research interests include the evaluation of psychotherapy outcomes with adolescents, and the relations between family interaction and child psychotherapy. Mailing address: Department of Psychology, University of Missouri, Columbia, MO 65211.

Barton J. Mann, MA, is a doctoral student in clinical psychology at the University of Missouri-Columbia. His areas of specialization include adolescent psychopathology, family relations, and family therapy.

Preparation of this article was supported in part by a grant from the University of Missouri-Columbia Research Council. We extend our appreciation and gratitude to Robert L. Perry of the Missouri Thirteenth Judicial Circuit Juvenile Court for his contributions to our clinical intervention study, and to the staff of the University of Missouri-Columbia Delinquency Project for their valuable ideas and support.

behavioral acting out; and a preoccupation with self, sexuality, and hedonism. This popular but inaccurate portrayal of adolescence has undoubtedly contributed to the view that psychotherapy with adolescents is a formidable task. Although adolescents evidence behavior problems that are quite different from those of younger and older patients, we have found that psychotherapy with adolescents does not need to be a long and arduous process. Nevertheless, we propose that some therapists have taken an unnecessarily narrow view of adolescent behavior problems and an overly restrictive approach to adolescent behavior change. In some cases, these limitations have led to therapeutic outcomes that have been viewed as disappointing (see, e.g., Borduin & Henggeler, 1982; Feldman, 1983).

In the development of effective, brief intervention strategies with adolescents, it is important to consider the multidimensional nature of adolescent behavior disorders. Indeed, researchers and theorists have reported that adolescent behavior is embedded within multiple interrelated social contexts including the family, the peer group, and the school system (Bronfenbrenner, 1979; Henggeler, 1982; O'Connor & Lubin, 1984). These social contexts exert an impact on the adolescent's behavior and are, in turn, influenced by the adolescent (Bell & Harper, 1977). Moreover, adolescents also possess individual characteristics that affect their behavior and the social systems in which they live.

One important individual characteristic that has a profound influence on the adolescent's behavior and social relations is his or her creative ability. Although there is continued debate over whether creativity represents a general ability or a domain-specific skill, there is increased recognition that excellence in a given area of accomplishment may offer a better basis for selecting adolescents for educational benefit than does testing for hidden creative abilities (Horowitz & O'Brien, 1985). From this perspective, adolescents' creative talents can be identified through their achievements in areas such as writing, science, the visual arts, drama, dance, or group leadership.

For some adolescents, the behaviors that are associated with creative talent can contribute to problems that require therapeutic interventions in one or more relevant systems. To date, however, there have been no attempts to describe the behavior problems of creative adolescents from a multisystemic model of adolescent psychosocial development. Furthermore, there are no articles in the literature regarding psychotherapeutic interventions with creative adolescents.

Accordingly, this article has two primary aims. First, we will describe some of the individual and systemic determinants of behavior problems in creative adolescents. Second, we will discuss a multi-systemic therapeutic approach we have developed and successfully used in the treatment of creative adolescents with behavior disorders.

THE SYSTEMIC CONTEXT
OF ADOLESCENT CREATIVITY:
EMPIRICAL DATA

Individual Characteristics

The cognitive skills that allow an adolescent to engage in divergent thinking have a strong impact on his or her overt behaviors. Researchers have found that creative adolescents are more outgoing, playful, and uninhibited in their social relations than are adolescents not identified as creative (Getzels & Jackson, 1961; Harrington, 1975). In addition, creative adolescents tend to be independent, nonconforming, confrontive, and critical of others (Bledsoe & Khatena, 1973; MacKinnon, 1962; Parloff, Datta, Kleman, & Handlon, 1968; Shaefer, 1970; Torrance, 1969). In some cases, the unrestrained and confrontive behaviors displayed by these adolescents may promote alienation and hostility from adults and peers. When this occurs, the adolescent may respond with deliberate efforts to antagonize these other persons. Such efforts, of course, only intensify the adolescent's interpersonal difficulties. Alternatively, the adolescent may suppress any divergent thoughts and behaviors in order to gain social acceptance. Unfortunately, by yielding to heavy pressures to conform, the adolescent may become overly dependent on others and may ignore his or her creative talents (Khatena, 1973). Thus, a major developmental task for creative adolescents is to strike a balance between their needs for social acceptance and the expression of their intrapersonal characteristics and abilities.

Family Relations

The most influential system in which creative adolescents are embedded is the family. However, it is important to recognize that creative adolescents also exert a significant influence on the behavior of other family members. As noted earlier, creative adolescents are often uninhibited, critical, and independent. Researchers have also found that these adolescents frequently possess high self-confidence and interpersonal sensitivity (Parloff et al., 1968; Schaefer, 1970). Collectively, these adolescent characteristics can lead the parents to believe that the adolescent has adult-like maturity and is capable of functioning autonomously. Consequently, it is not surprising to find that parents of creative adolescents are more permissive, less restrictive, and less consistent in their discipline practices than are parents of adolescents not identified as creative (Dewing, 1970; MacKinnon, 1962; Rejskind, 1982). However, for the adolescent to successfully emancipate from the family, the parents must provide guidance and set appropriate limits on the adolescent's behavior (Ackerman, 1980; Olson, Sprenkle, & Russell, 1979; Rodick & Henggeler, 1982). If the parents do not retain ultimate control, the adolescent is likely to engage in irresponsible behaviors that may lead to long-term psychosocial problems.

The creative adolescent may also attempt to "play one parent against the other" to achieve virtually unlimited freedom within the family. This is especially likely to occur if the parents have marital difficulties. Indeed, creative adolescents are frequently adept at detecting interpersonal difficulties (e.g., marital tension). Should the adolescent succeed in his or her efforts to promote interparental conflict about childrearing strategies, it is unlikely that either parent will successfully control the adolescent's behavior. Although the parents may recognize that the adolescent is engaged in a number of problematic behaviors outside the home, the parents' continued disagreement over parenting strategies may prevent an effective solution to the adolescent's problem behaviors.

Adolescents also need secure emotional relationships with their parents in order to successfully emancipate. Emancipation involves alternately moving away from the parents to test out interpersonal skills in the world of peers and returning to parents for emotional support and nurturance. However, in families with a creative adolescent, the parents may view the adolescent's pursuit of autonomy and self-determination in terms of a low need for affection or as outright rejection. In such cases, the parents may withdraw affection or may show negative affect toward the adolescent. In turn, the adolescent may interpret the parents' emotional distance or negativity as a rejection of his or her attempts to individuate. In support of this conceptualization, there is evidence that parents of creative adolescents are more detached and less warm in their relations with the adolescent than are parents of noncreative adolescents (MacKinnon, 1962; Schaefer, 1970; Weisberg & Springer, 1961). In families where marital difficulties also exist, the parents may compete for the adolescent's affection. Unfortunately, as in cases where the adolescent is rejected by both parents, interparental competition for the adolescent's affection is likely to impede the adolescent's attempts to emancipate and may result in serious behavior problems. For example, the adolescent may engage in promiscuous sexual behavior or drug use in an effort to obtain a consistent source of affection from peers.

Extrafamilial Systems

One system that becomes especially influential during adolescence is the peer group. Although adolescents identify more strongly with their parents than with peers (Rutter, 1980), adolescents conform more with peers when making decisions regarding everyday living. In addition, the peer group provides a source of self-esteem, emotional support, and information regarding appropriate and valued behavior in different situations (Panella, Cooper, & Henggeler, 1982). Hence, an adolescent's peers can have a strong impact upon behaviors such as drug use (Brook, Whiteman, & Gordon, 1983), sexual activity (Jorgensen, King, & Torrey, 1980), and involvement in illegal activities (Hanson, Henggeler, Haefele, & Rodick, 1984). Moreover, there is evidence to suggest that in families where discipline is inconsistent, the adolescent is even more susceptible to the influence of delinquent peers (e.g., Poole & Regoli, 1979).

As described earlier, creative adolescents possess certain characteristics that may lead to rejection by a number of their peers. In an attempt to satisfy their needs for emotional support and acceptance, these adolescents may become involved with peer groups that tolerate and even encourage deviant behavior. However, to the extent that the adolescent's peer group engages in behavior that conflicts with societal norms (e.g., drug use, delinquency), maintaining a membership within such a peer group may entail long-term negative consequences for the creative adolescent.

The school environment also affects the behavior of the creative adolescent. Because of the highly structured and routine nature of many classroom tasks, creative children and adolescents often become bored and restless (Wallach & Kogan, 1965). In an attempt to make things more interesting for themselves and their classmates, these adolescents may engage in playful yet disruptive behavior. From a systems perspective, this behavior serves an adaptive function for the adolescent. However, this behavior also entails some obvious risks and costs. For example, if the teacher fails to recognize the reasons behind the adolescent's behavior, the adolescent may draw the teacher into an infuriating power struggle. Should this occur, it is likely that the adolescent will be referred to the school principal or guidance counselor. Although we would like to report that these referrals typically result in a positive and efficient solution to the creative adolescent's classroom difficulties, we have found that such solutions are relatively rare. If the adolescent is not temporarily suspended from school, he or she will probably be required to attend meetings with the school counselor. In either event, the respite from the classroom may actually reinforce the adolescent's disruptive behavior and may eventually lead to academic failure. Thus, if the adolescent is to succeed in the classroom, an accurate appraisal of the factors that are maintaining the adolescent's problem behaviors is necessary.

In summary, it seems essential to consider the transactions of the creative adolescent within several pertinent systems when analyzing the parameters of behavior problems. It is clear that the variables within these domains frequently interact with each other to influence problem behaviors. For example, in an effort to evade the consequences of disruptive classroom behavior, the adolescent may use one system (e.g., parents) to undermine the other (e.g., school). Similarly, the adolescent's problematic relations with peers may be linked to certain individual characteristics.

We now turn our attention to a therapeutic approach that has been developed to address the multidimensional nature of adolescent behavior problems. We will discuss how this approach can be applied to the treatment of problem behaviors in creative adolescents and their families.

THE FAMILY-ECOLOGICAL SYSTEMS APPROACH

During the past eight years, the family-ecological systems approach has been evaluated in three controlled outcome studies with approximately 300 behavior problem adolescents and their families (see e.g., Henggeler et al., 1986). This treatment approach is based primarily on theory and research findings within the fields of family therapy, developmental psychology, and child-clinical psychology. The family-ecological systems approach does not stress novel therapeutic techniques, but instead offers an integrative and comprehensive conceptual framework from which to view the multidimensional determinants of adolescent behavior. Using this framework, the clinician decides which systems are most dysfunctional and choses therapeutic techniques that are targeted at the identified dysfunction.

The systems that are most commonly targeted for intervention in the family-ecological approach are the individual, the family, the peer group, and the school. Interventions might focus on one of these systems, on several systems, or on the relations between systems. For example, marital therapy, family therapy, teacher or parent-teacher consultation, peer group intervention, and self-control training might each be appropriate in a particular case. Although each case is unique and receives a set of interventions that are highly specific to that case, we have found that certain intervention tactics and strategies are particularly effective with behavior-problem adolescents who are highly creative.

Individual Characteristics

Traditional approaches to the treatment of adolescent behavior problems have focused almost exclusively on the remediation of deficits in the individual adolescent. Although these remedial efforts may be needed to help the adolescent function effectively in certain life areas, we do not believe that the remediation of behavioral deficits should represent the sole thrust of therapy with adolescents. In fact, we have found that by helping adolescents identify and build on their existing strengths, these strengths can often be effectively used to promote positive change.

Creative adolescents frequently possess a number of significant talents, yet these adolescents do not necessarily exercise their talents, nor do they necessarily receive recognition and support for using their talents. Thus, one therapeutic strategy that is frequently useful is to provide the creative adolescent with assistance in the development and utilization of his or her superior abilities. Adolescents with musical talents can be encouraged to participate in organized musical groups (e.g., the school jazz band); artistically creative adolescents can be introduced to, and even employed by, successful artists in the community; adolescents with literary talents can be assisted in joining the staff of the school newspaper; mechanically talented adolescents can be enrolled in special vocational programs and can work as apprentices in certain employment settings; and athletically gifted youth can be paired with local college athletic standouts and encouraged to participate in organized sports. These activities provide socially appropriate outlets for the adolescent's creative talents and frequently serve as a source of pride and stimulation. Moreover, to the extent that the parent(s) can be encouraged to assist the adolescent in developing his or her creative talents, it is often possible to open lines of parent-adolescent communication and to increase positive reciprocity between the parent(s) and adolescent.

Some creative adolescents have idiosyncratic interpersonal styles that do not promote positive relations with peers and teachers. With these adolescents, social-skills interventions that include role plays, practice in perspective-taking, and instruction in conflict resolution can be quite effective in improving the adolescents' interpersonal relations. Because creative adolescents are often intelligent and insightful, education and advice about interpersonal relations may be all that are needed in some cases. In other cases, however, the adolescent may have poor impulse control. Inasmuch as difficulties in self-control can seriously interfere with social development, academic performance, and the productive use of creative abilities, it is important that these difficulties be remediated as quickly and efficiently as possible. We have found that creative adolescents who evidence problems in self-control are ideal candidates for cognitive self-instructional training. This training teaches the adolescent to generate several alternative courses of action and to weigh the likely consequences of each alternative before deciding on a given response (see Kendall & Braswell, 1985; Spivack, Platt, & Shure, 1976; Williams & Akamatsu, 1978).

It is important to note that the successful implementation of individually based treatment strategies with the creative adolescent requires that the therapist develop a trusting, supportive relationship with the adolescent. The therapist must be willing to invest substantial time and energy in developing rapport, and must be flexible enough to tolerate and to appreciate the creative adolescent's imaginative yet sometimes aggravating forms of self-expression. Once a trusting relationship has been established, the therapist can exert the needed leverage to effect positive change in the adolescent's behavior.

Family Relations

The association between family relations and adolescent behavior is well-documented. Indeed, many adolescent behavior problems are direct reflections of marital difficulties (Emery, 1982) and ineffective discipline strategies (Olweus, 1980). Although our interventions with behavior-problem adolescents usually include some form of family therapy, we have found that it is seldom useful to challenge the parents' definition of the presenting problem (i.e., the adolescent's behavior) or to redefine the problem in terms of marital difficulties. Parents who seek professional assistance for their problem adolescent typically feel blameworthy and incompetent and, in our view, do not need to have additional blame heaped onto them by the therapist. Moreover, if the therapist alienates the parents, the likelihood of therapeutic success is significantly reduced. To obtain parental cooperation and support for various therapeutic interventions, it is usually best if the therapist overtly accepts the parents' definition of the "problem." To counteract the parents' feelings of self-blame, the therapist can point out competent parental behaviors (e.g., providing for the adolescent's physical needs, coming to therapy) and label these behaviors as demonstrations of concern for the adolescent's welfare. Once the parents feel that the therapist understands and appreciates their predicament, they are more likely to follow the therapist's suggestions for helping the problem adolescent. Depending on the factors that are maintaining the adolescent's behavior, the therapist might use a variety of techniques to (a) promote more appropriate discipline strategies, (b) develop positive parent-adolescent relations, and/or (c) resolve underlying marital conflicts.

Therapeutic interventions in the families of creative adolescents often involve teaching the parents more appropriate discipline strategies. In most instances, the therapist must initially counsel the parents concerning the adolescent's needs for guidance and for models of responsible adult behavior. The parents may also need to be reminded of their responsibility to, as well as for, their adolescent child. The therapist can then educate the parents in the use of control strategies that are consistent with the adolescent's developmental level. Often, however, the parent's initial disciplinary efforts will be met by an increase in the adolescent's noxious behavior. Thus, the therapist must alert the parents to the likelihood of adolescent resistance and must provide them with substantial and continued support in their attempts to correct the adolescent. Given such support, the therapist can frequently help the parents return to a position of leadership within the family.

Emotional warmth is perhaps the most important dimension of parent-adolescent relations. In families with creative adolescents, however, the parents may believe that the adolescent does not need continued expressions of parental nurturance, or they may be unsure of developmentally appropriate ways to express such nurturance. When such difficulties are observed, it is important to teach the family members appropriate ways to give and receive affection. To accomplish this task, the therapist should attempt to describe the needed changes in a way that arouses minimal defensiveness on the part of the relevant family members. For example, in the case of an intellectually gifted, physically diminutive adolescent boy who was referred for stealing money from his emotionally distant father, the second author (BJM) explained to the family that the son needed the father's praise to feel secure about his masculinity and to make the transition into manhood. The family was also told that the son needed to spend more time with the father in order to learn about the father's employment experiences and to ask for the father's input about part-time employment opportunities. A number of joint activities were then planned that were designed to promote positive reciprocity in the father-son dyad.

Marital difficulties can also play a significant role in the maintenance of deviant adolescent behavior. However, with the therapist's assistance, the parents can frequently agree not to subvert each other's authority, and to provide disciplinary consistency. In many families, a strengthening of the parental coalition may be sufficient to stop the creative adolescent's deviant behavior and to facilitate adolescent psychosocial functioning. Nevertheless, when the adolescent's behavior problems have abated, one or both parents may express a desire to increase their marital satisfaction. When this occurs, the therapist can offer to shift the focus of therapy to the marriage. If both of the parents are committed to seeking improvement in the marriage, the shift to marital therapy can often consolidate changes that have been made in the adolescent's behavior. However, if either of the parents declines to participate in marital therapy, it is usually not advisable for the therapist to force the issue. Instead, the therapist can remind the parents of the impact that marital disagreement has on the adolescent's behavior and can leave open the option of marital therapy as a future possibility.

Extrafamilial Systems

Although the family system often represents an important focus within family-ecological therapy, it is not the only system in which to intervene to remediate dysfunctional adolescent behavior. From an initial focus on the individual adolescent and the family, interventions may also extend to peer, school, and other community systems, and to the relations between the systems.

Teachers and parents can often provide useful information about the creative adolescent's peer group activities and about the attitudes and adjustment of peer group members. When either of these sources indicates that the adolescent is embedded within a deviant peer group, it is important to perform a direct assessment of the adolescent's peer relations. Without such an assessment, it is difficult to determine the peer group's potential for change and, thus, to plan realistic and effective interventions. Direct assessment of the peer group system can also help the therapist to understand the adolescent's behavior in both the family and school systems.

For obvious reasons, direct assessment of the adolescent's peer group is difficult to accomplish in the absence of a trusting relationship between the adolescent and therapist. After such a relationship has been established, the next step generally involves arranging a number of informal meetings with the adolescent and his or her friends. This step can be accomplished in various ways depending on the interests of both the adolescent and the therapist. For example, the therapist might ask the adolescent to invite several friends to participate in a mutually enjoyed activity (e.g., basketball, video games, shopping). If such an activity cannot be arranged, it is often possible for the therapist to have informal conversations with the adolescent and some friends at a place and time when the peer group is usually together (e.g., after school at a local fast food restaurant). Whatever the setting, it is usually not difficult for the therapist to meet the adolescent's peers and to assess their attitudes and interaction patterns.

In many cases, the therapist is likely to find that the creative adolescent's behavior problems (e.g., stealing) are reinforced by the attitudes and behaviors of peers. Nevertheless, the therapist may be able to effect behavioral changes among the adolescent and his or her peers by assisting them in obtaining desired goals (e.g., job skills training, employment, a sponsor for a sports team or musical group). In such instances, the peer group can continue to provide the adolescent with a sense of self-worth and security without promoting deviant behavioral norms. In some instances, however, the therapist may judge that the peer group's potential for positive change is minimal. If the adolescent is motivated to change his or her behavior (e.g., drug use), the therapist can teach the adolescent effective ways to cope with peer pressures. Or, the therapist (and parents) might advocate withdrawal from the present peer group and encourage an affiliation with nonproblem peers. This latter intervention is more likely to succeed if the nonproblem peers have creative talents and interests that are similar to those of the target adolescent.

To obtain a clear understanding of the adolescent's classroom and school performance, it is critical that the therapist conducts an assessment of the adolescent's cognitive functioning and attitudes toward school. A meeting with several of the adolescent's teachers might also provide valuable information about the adolescent's academic strengths and weaknesses, classroom behavior, and relations with school personnel. After obtaining this information, the therapist can then decide whether interventions are needed within the school system and, if so, the exact form that these interventions should take.

A detailed description of the various intervention strategies that could be implemented in the school setting cannot be accomplished within the present space limitations. For example, if the therapist finds that the creative adolescent has a learning disability, extensive academic training and vocational planning would be needed. However, the school system interventions that we have used most frequently with creative adolescents follow directly from our discussion of the academic difficulties that are most common in this population. The first step in school intervention usually involves persuading the creative adolescent that success in school is necessary to achieve a number of important goals in life. Indeed, we believe that it is extremely important that each child achieve up to his or her capabilities because success in school sets the tone for future peer relations and socioeconomic opportunities. If the adolescent has not already established some vocational or educational goals, the parents can be encouraged to assist the adolescent in this process. In most cases, it is also helpful if the adolescent's satisfactory achievement and behavior in school are linked to some short-term objectives (e.g., obtaining a part-time job, receiving an allowance).

Once the adolescent's cooperation has been obtained, the therapist can help the adolescent to appreciate the impact that his or her classroom disruptions have on the feelings and professional relations of the teacher(s). The adolescent can also be helped to recognize the long-term disadvantages of antagonizing influential members of the school hierarchy. Since the creative adolescent is capable of understanding and predicting the teacher's responses to socially desirable behavior, the therapist can coach the adolescent regarding ways to create positive expectancies and to eliminate negative ones. For example, the adolescent can initiate friendly greetings at appropriate times, complete homework assignments early, and ask questions about content areas that he or she does not understand.

The therapist can also meet with the teachers to discuss the adolescent's creative talents and the adolescent's desire to improve in the classroom. In addition, the teachers can be asked for suggestions about the development of the adolescent's creativity. Thus, the therapist serves as an advocate for the adolescent and attempts to promote feelings of positive regard between the teachers and adolescent. By intervening in this manner, it is possible to make the school experience more varied and challenging for the creative adolescent.

Interactions Between Systems

In some instances, the therapist may also need to provide interventions that target the transactions between two or more systems. A common focus is the interface between family and school. The parents may feel that their child is being persecuted by his or her teachers, and the teachers may feel that the parents are unsupportive of the school's efforts to correct the adolescent's problem behavior. Accordingly, an important therapeutic goal is to open intersystem communication channels and gain collaboration on mutually desired goals. Initially, the therapist takes responsibility for bringing the parents and teachers together and mediates parent-teacher interactions so that mutual goals can be established. Often, parent-teacher cooperation can be established through the use of a daily homework assignment sheet for the adolescent that is signed by both parties. The parents can also call the teacher at scheduled times to check on the adolescent's behavioral progress. During this process, the therapist should monitor the participation of parents and teachers and should regularly provide reinforcement for continued cooperation.

The therapist can also assist the family members in their transactions with other community systems. For example, in low-income families, the therapist may need to teach the parents to successfully negotiate the social-service maze to obtain needed services for the adolescent or a sibling. In single-parent families, the therapist can encourage the parent to become involved in support groups (e.g., Parents Without Partners) and educational programs that are designed to meet the specific needs that many parents face following divorce.

CONCLUSION

Adolescent creativity is related to numerous individual and systemic variables in the adolescent's ecological environment. Each of these variables can influence the behavior of the creative adolescent and can play an important role in the emergence and maintenance of psychosocial problems. In providing treatment to disturbed adolescents with creative talents, careful consideration of the adolescent's family-ecological context seems a therapeutic necessity. Failure to consider the potential impact and interaction of the systemic variables that have been shown to affect adolescent behavior may result in treatment interventions that are ineffective.

The role of the therapist is an apt summary of the family-ecological systems approach as used with creative adolescents. The family-ecological systems therapist must have a broad knowledge of community resources and institutions, must be familiar with a wide range of therapeutic techniques, and, above all, must participate as an active member of the adolescent's social environment. Indeed, family-ecological systems therapy requires that the therapist obtain a comprehensive understanding of the creative adolescent and his or her systems. The therapist can then provide systemic interventions that eliminate the need for the problem behaviors and encourage the development of the adolescent's creative talents.

REFERENCES

Ackerman, N. J. (1980). The family with adolescents. In E. A. Carter & M. McGoldrick (Eds.), *The family life cycle* (pp. 147-170). New York: Gardner Press.

Bell, R. Q., & Harper, L. V. (1977). *Child effects on adults.* Hillsdale, NJ: Erlbaum.

Bledsoe, J. C., & Khatena, J. (1973). Factor analytic study of Something About Myself. *Psychological Reports, 32,* 1176-1178.

Borduin, C. M., & Henggeler, S. W. (1982). Treating the family of the adolescent: A review of the empirical literature. In S. W. Henggeler (Ed.), *Delinquency and adolescent psychopathology: A family-ecological systems approach* (pp. 205-222). Littleton, MA: Wright-PSG.

Bronfenbrenner, U. (1979). *The ecology of human development.* Cambridge, MA: Harvard University Press.

Brook, J. S., Whiteman, M., & Gordon, A. S. (1983). Stages of drug use in adolescence: Personality, peer, and family correlates. *Developmental Psychology, 199,* 269-277.

Dewing, K. (1970). Family influences on creativity: A review and discussion. *Journal of Special Education, 4,* 399-404.

Emery, R. L. (1982). Interparental conflict and the children of discord and divorce. *Psychological Bulletin, 92,* 310-330.

Feldman, P. (1983). Juvenile offending: Behavioral approaches to prevention and intervention. *Child and Family Behavior Therapy, 5,* 37-50.

Getzels, J. W., & Jackson, P. W. (1961). Family environment and cognitive style: A study of the sources of highly intelligent and highly creative adolescents. *American Sociological Review, 26,* 351-359.

Hanson, C. L., Henggeler, S. W., Haefele, W. F., & Rodick, J. D. (1984). Demographic, individual, and family relationship correlates of serious and repeated crime among adolescents and their siblings. *Journal of Consulting and Clinical Psychology, 52,* 528-538.

Harrington, D. M. (1975). Effects of explicit instructions to "be creative" on the psychological meaning of divergent thinking test scores. *Journal of Personality, 43,* 434-454.

Henggeler, S. W. (Ed.). (1982). *Delinquency and adolescent psychopathology: A family-ecological systems approach.* Littleton, MA: Wright-PSG.

Henggeler, S. W.., Rodick, J. D., Borduin, C. M., Hanson, C. L., Watson, S. M., & Urey, J. R. (1986). Multisystemic treatment of juvenile offenders: Effects on adolescent behavior and family interaction. *Developmental Psychology, 22,* 132-141.

Horowitz, F. D., & O'Brien, M. (Eds.). (1985). *The gifted and talented: Developmental perspectives.* Washington, DC: American Psychological Association.

Jorgensen, S. R., King, S. L., & Torrey, B. A. (1980). Dyadic and social network influences on adolescent exposure of pregnancy risk. *Journal of Marriage and the Family, 42,* 141-155.

Kendall, P. C., & Braswell, L. (1985). *Cognitive-behavioral therapy for impulsive children.* New York: Guilford.

Khatena, J. (1974). Parents and the creatively gifted. *Gifted Child Quarterly, 18,* 202-209.

MacKinnon, D. W. (1962). The nature and nurture of creative talent. *American Psychologist, 17,* 484-495.

O'Connor, W. A., & Lubin, B. (Eds.). (1984). *Ecological approaches to clinical and community psychology.* New York: Wiley.

Olson, D. H., Sprenkle, D., & Russell, C. (1979). Circumplex model of marital and family systems: I. Cohesion and adaptability dimensions, family types, and clinical applications. *Family Process, 18,* 3-28.

Olweus, D. (1980). Familial and temperamental determinants of aggressive behavior in adolescent boys: A causal analysis. *Developmental Psychology, 16,* 644-660.

Panella, D. H., Cooper, P. F., & Henggeler, S. W. (1982). Peer relations in adolescence. In S. W. Henggeler (Ed.), *Delinquency and adolescent psychopathology: A family-ecological systems approach* (pp. 139-161). Littleton, MA: Wright-PSG.

Parloff, M. B., Datta, L., Kleman, M., & Handlon, J. H. (1968). Personality characteristics which differentiate creative male adolescents and adults. *Journal of Personality, 36,* 528-552.

Poole, E. D., & Regoli, R. M. (1979). Parental support, delinquent friends, and delinquency: A test of interaction effects. *Journal of Criminal Law and Criminology, 700,* 188-193.

Rejskind, F. G. (1982). Autonomy and creativity in children. *Journal of Creative Behavior, 16,* 58-67.

Rodick, J. D., & Henggeler, S. W. (1982). Parent-child interaction and adolescent emancipation. In S. W. Henggeler (Ed.), *Delinquency and adolescent psychopathology: A family-ecological systems approach* (pp. 43-67). Littleton, MA: Wright-PSG.

Rutter, M. (1980). *Changing youth in a changing society: Patterns of adolescent development and disorder.* Cambridge, MA: Harvard University Press.

Schaefer, C. E. (1970). A psychological study of 120 exceptionally creative adolescent girls. *Exceptional Children, 36,* 431-441.

Spivack, G., Platt, J., & Shure, M. (1976). *The problem-solving approach to adjustment.* San Francisco: Jossey-Bass.

Torrance, E. P. (1969). *Creativity.* San Rafael, CA: Dimensions.

Wallach, M. A., & Kogan, N. (1965). *Modes of thinking in children: A study of the creativity-intelligence distinction.* New York: Holt, Rinehart & Winston.

Weisberg, P. S., & Springer, K. J. (1961). Environmental factors in creative function. *Archives of General Psychiatry, 5,* 64-74.

Williams, D., & Akamatsu, T. (1978). Cognitive self-guidance training with juvenile delinquents: Applications and generalization. *Cognitive Therapy and Research, 2,* 285-288.

Psychotherapy with Creative People: Dismantling the Roadblocks

Jeffery C. Hutzler
Daniel S. P. Schubert

SUMMARY. This article identifies several problems that occur in psychotherapy with the creative patient. These problems center on preconceived beliefs on the part of the patient and of the psychotherapist. Such difficulties need to be made explicit at the outset of therapy and dealt with repeatedly as psychotherapy progresses, or progress may be blocked. The authors support the belief that psychotherapy stimulates creativity. They also discuss common themes found during psychotherapy with a creative person and strategies for dealing with these themes.

Many creative people enter into psychotherapy. Usually these people have some problem they are trying to solve. They are anxious, depressed; have writer's block, or some other symptom or group of symptoms. Some of these people know what their problem is, but others do not.

Choosing the appropriate therapeutic approach for these people requires the psychotherapist to formulate a problem. However, it also requires a special understanding of the creative person. There are particular problems in treating the creative person both in terms of understanding that particular individual, and also in terms of the psychotherapist's own personality.

Freud (1963) thought that artists were often neurotic. This led to the pervasive belief that artists produced an artwork—whether it

Jeffery C. Hutzler, MD, is with the Department of Psychiatry of the Cleveland Clinic Foundation. Mailing address: Department of Psychiatry, Cleveland Clinic Foundation, 9500 Euclid Ave., Cleveland, OH 44106.

Daniel S. P. Schubert, MD, PhD, is affiliated with the School of Medicine, Case Western Reserve University, and the Department of Psychiatry, Metropolitan General Hospital, Cleveland, OH 44109.

was a novel, poetry, visual art, or music—as a result of a neurotic conflict. Research does not support this belief. It is likely that creative people tolerate conflict better, often, than less creative people (Arieti, 1976; Storr, in press; Flach, in press).

Creative patients usually are attempting to organize abstract thought or their own vision of their environment. In this manner, creative people are frequently adept at organizing disparate parts into a whole in one form or another. This attribute makes creative people excellent candidates for psychotherapy, since they are already adept at problem solving and at unifying seemingly unrelated parts. Creative people are good problem solvers and usually are average or above average in intelligence. It has become evident that intelligence is certainly a necessary part of the creative process, but it is also clear that raw intelligence does not produce creativity in itself (Schubert DSP, 1973).

Creative patients may be creative in at least two ways. They may be creative in problem solving, or they may be creative in the arts. People who solve problems as a form of creativity are able to come up with many more solutions to a presented problem than are their less creative counterparts. Artistic creativity, of course, is more difficult to measure because the judge is often the limiting factor in this decision. Thus, the statement that "beauty is in the eye of the beholder" is a summary of the achievement and frustration an artist must face in creating.

Creative patients, therefore, are often intelligent, resourceful, used to dealing with ambiguity, and are often good problem solvers. This should make this group of patients an interesting and enjoyable group with whom to work. There are, however, certain problems that can diminish the impact of psychotherapy in these patients.

ROADBLOCKS TO THERAPY

The creative patient may bring a number of biases to psychotherapy which can interfere with the process of treatment. One of these beliefs is that the person involved in creative work may become more conventional, as a result of psychotherapy, and his or her work will suffer thereby. It is a commonly held belief that a good deal of creative output is the product of neurotic conflict, as we have mentioned. Thus, the creative patient may believe that solving such neurotic conflicts will result in a decreased creative productivity and a more conventional view of the world.

Creative people also fear that the psychotherapist may lack an understanding of their special needs and abilities. They may believe that the psychotherapist is a representative of "conventional society" and will not be able to put them in a proper perspective. The creative patient then often enters psychotherapy with important concerns about the outcome of psychotherapy, as well as the psychotherapist's own personality and beliefs. These can be important roadblocks to psychotherapy unless they are made explicit early in treatment and dealt with thoroughly and repeatedly.

REMOVING THESE ROADBLOCKS

Certainly the creative patient needs to be reassured that creativity is not squelched by psychotherapy. In fact, it has been shown that conventionally thinking and conformist people tend not to be creative (Barron, 1963). In fact, creativity is often stimulated by psychotherapy, giving rise to a richer and more intense awareness of internal psychological life. It also may enhance the complexity with which the patient sees interpersonal relationships. As an example, a young writer who developed writer's block may find that he or she is still rebelling against father's authoritarian personality.

The writer is not able to produce creative material in response to self-imposed deadlines or to those of a publisher. During psychotherapy, it becomes clear to this creative author that a whole world of complex relationships has been closed off to him or her and is manifesting itself in seemingly bothersome symptoms. This gives rise to a whole fabric of new material that can be applied both in the patient's self-understanding and may also appear in the content of the writing. The writer may find, for example, that rebellion, as a theme, becomes important in his or her writing or in a major character.

At the outset of psychotherapy, it should be made clear to the patient that the psychotherapist has a bias that psychotherapy is supportive of the creative process. It will become clear immediately to the patient within the first few sessions (he or she may be reassured) that autobiographical material reviewed in psychotherapy gives a clearer understanding of the patient's symptoms, and also provides material for further productivity and richer themes upon which to elaborate. As an example, as a painter became aware that his Italian immigrant father drank alcohol heavily in order to express strong negative or positive feelings, he became aware of his own sense of release in the nonverbal but intense production of his painting. This enhanced his productivity, since he was able to confront painful feelings and thoughts about his own family, and rather than becoming depressed and helpless, he painted more vigorously. As he admitted to his feelings, they became more available to him. It reinforced the idea that talking about his thoughts and feelings about his past actually stirred up intense feelings, which acted as stimuli for further productivity, rather than causing him to feel confused and frustrated.

During psychotherapy with the creative patient, discussion should be encouraged about the patient's fears of being misunderstood by the therapist. Many artistic and creative people feel that they are "different" as part of their persona. This tends to be reinforced in adolescence and early adulthood by group identification and exclusion of others with dissimilar beliefs. Because the therapist, for instance, wears a coat and tie, the patient may feel a surge of suspicion. Transference issues such as these, however, are a rich source of creative stimulus for the patient. They can elucidate extremely interesting processes within the creative person. The creative patient will come to see that the therapeutic relationship can be seen as a microcosm of a larger world in which the patient and therapist live. Interesting and even fantastic themes can be talked about openly and comfortably within this protected setting. This gives rise to an enhanced ability to free-associate and follow fantasy and reality as it intertwines in discussions of the patient's past and present emotional life. This may allow the creative patient to trace his or her "differentness" from early childhood on. During this time, he or she may also begin to recognize that this sense of "differentness" can also give rise to extremely acute powers of observation as is always developed in someone who "stands aside" and watched processes in institutions and interpersonal relationships.

USEFUL STRATEGIES WITH A CREATIVE PATIENT

It is helpful to review, at the beginning of psychotherapy with a creative patient, the psychotherapist's own bias that creativity should be encouraged by therapy. It should also be noted that the therapist is ready to stand out of the way, when the patient improves with or without the help of the therapist. This allays fears in the patient that the therapist has a hidden agenda or a rigid outcome expectation. This will encourage the patient to become more involved in creative problem-solving in his own life. The psychotherapist can follow the lead of the patient as a model in pursuing the patient's own demons. As an example, if a patient brings in a unique and intriguing view of his drive in a car to the therapist's office, which he views as a "battle of wills with other drivers," this may be used in the context of psychotherapy as it relates to power struggles, sexual themes, and aggression. As the patient sees that the psychotherapist can seize upon and use interesting and seemingly anecdotal but creative views of the world, he or she will bring more of them into therapy and both the therapist and patient will benefit.

It is also possible that the psychotherapist may deal with periodically psychotic creative people. It may be important early in psychotherapy to reassure the patient that the therapist will identify and comment on inappropriate material that may be self-destructive to the patient. For instance, if a patient has periodic paranoid thinking, the therapist needs to identify and isolate this process from the ongoing function of the patient's daily life with other people. In fact, utilizing this material in one's creative productivity may actually help to encapsulate and isolate it from the patient's everyday life and therefore distance one from it. This allows the patient a sense of intellectual and emotional mastery, which can improve self-esteem and functioning. Therefore, this creative patient may benefit from painting or writing about paranoid themes as a way of developing a healthier observing ego.

It may be that, from time to time, the therapist needs to reevaluate the course of therapy with the creative patient. Creative patients may introduce so many interesting and rich themes that the central theme or themes of psychotherapy are lost or never finished. It is important, therefore, not to get scattered but to elect to pursue one, two, or three different themes in psychotherapy until their central conflict or problems are solved. Some very creative people may bring in a steady stream of interesting themes that are not necessarily related and cause confusion and a lack of focus in therapy. There are two methods to deal with this problem. One is to relate most of these diverse themes to one major "executive theme" so that therapy proceeds around a central idea. The other method is to mention that each of these new themes is an interesting one but "let's finish with a couple of the other major issues before we get on to that one."

Intellectualizing is certainly a seductive "red herring" to get into in psychotherapy, particularly with a creative patient. This is another reason to attempt to maintain a central theme in therapy when possible. As part of this process, avoiding intense emotional issues, a patient may bring in a book or article to discuss with the therapist rather than dealing with the therapist's interpretation (Hutzler & Pinta, 1977).

In this vein, too, it is also helpful to choose therapy issues to work on that are treatable and probably will result in some closure. Therefore, avoiding certain processes that are draining and tend to prevent the flow of therapy is helpful. Thus, severely obsessive or intellectualized themes may need to be avoided. In order to do this, the patient needs to be encouraged to accept emotional productions as he or she brings them to therapy. Discouraging an overly intellectualized or obsessional approach to psychotherapy is usually helpful. It is rarely true, however, that the opposite is the case. If the patient, therefore, is unable to organize himself or herself and needs to be carefully structured during therapy, obviously intellectual mastery may be called upon. Being flexible and able to respond with a repertoire of behavior on the part of the therapist is important. It may be that a "B type" therapist may be more helpful with "healthy" creative patients. This kind of therapist allows the direction to be set by the patient, has little structure during the hour, and is nondirective. On the other hand, an "A type" therapist, who tends to be more structured, directive, and supportive, may be more helpful in treating creative people with distorted thinking or disruptive mood swings, such as schizophrenic, bipolar, or borderline patients (Schubert, in press).

Nonetheless, the major trend in treating creative patients is undoubtedly in the direction of enhancing their own awareness of interesting and idiosyncratic feelings within themselves. This stimulates further creativity, tends to give more shape to the core or theme, and thus its eventual incorporation and solution. Therefore, if a young male poet senses that he is being watched by "evil figures" in the woods beyond his house, it would be the most helpful to explore this further, rather than helping the patient to deny and cover up the symptom. In this particular case, such uncovering therapy in this schizophrenic patient resulted in his ability to identify the onset of a paranoid process early, so that he could adjust his medication and work with his therapist more intensely, thus avoiding repeated psychotic episodes requiring hospitalization. It also made him aware of feelings of anger toward his mother, who was being periodically overprotective.

It is also helpful for the psychotherapist to recognize that certain personality characteristics are less malleable than neurotic issues. For instance, if a patient has shown a highly compulsive personality style all of his or her life, it is unlikely that this will change appreciably. Therefore, choosing more whimsical and impulsive thought patterns and feelings to deal with in therapy would be more productive both for the therapist and for the patient in the expansion of the latter's ability to be creative. In this vein, it is also important to work with interpersonal issues that block creativity. As an example, the extremely oversensitive patient may have difficulty in making and maintaining relationships. This causes some isolation and decreases the numbers of interpersonal interactions and relationships, and therefore decreases the potential for creative interactions. The same would be true of patients who are extremely suspicious, competitive, and so on. Reality, therefore, must remain the basis for psychotherapy, though the elaborations on reality are what often make it most interesting.

Finally, it is important not to fear playfulness and the use of mirth and humor in psychotherapy with creative people. Certainly, there is a childlike quality in this that enhances creativity. Humor is based upon seeing absurdities and incongruities of everyday life. This is a rich stimulation for creative thinking. The therapist, of course, needs to be able to enjoy the patient, and by encouraging humor and a sense of the absurd when it is appropriate, the patient and therapist both thrive.

COMMON THEMES IN THE CREATIVE PATIENT

Many artists have a great need for acceptance of their productions. They may have difficulty admitting this, but validation of their artwork by public acceptance is important. This public acceptance may be very small and limited to a few people but is often required for the artist to go on. The process of communicating with others validates the individual, as an artist, rather than someone with idiosyncratic and insignificant ideas (Kris, 1952; Stein & Flach [Eds.], in press). Underlying these needs, of course, in a creative person, are themes of narcissism. It may be important to explore the roles of grandiosity and dependency that the creative person had as an infant and adolescent. He or she may not have fused these two poles, which may give rise to difficulty finishing artworks. Feelings of dependency and entitlement without working to completion may interfere with assertiveness and completion of ideas in the form of a painting, a poem, a movie, and so on (Kubie, 1958). As the patient then learns to integrate flights into extreme independence, vacillating with feelings of many unmet dependency needs, he or she will be able to be more productive and consistent, and certainly no less creative.

Certainly, themes of gender are important in treating creative people. Most creative people have strong masculine and feminine characteristics and are able to effectively integrate them both (Dellas & Gaier, 1970). The creative process often requires the ability to enter into and to understand both masculine and feminine roles and feelings. Resolving some of the natural conflict patients may have about this will allow the patient to use this increased repertoire more effectively, rather than dampen his or her creativity. It usually allows more integration of the ego in a healthier way, also providing for a better self-esteem and interpersonal function. This may indeed be why creative people often rate better on tests of ego strength than do noncreative people (Schubert & Flach [Eds.], in press).

PROBLEMS FOR THE THERAPIST

Competition with the patient can be a problem for many creative psychotherapists. It is obvious that we need to examine our own needs and feelings constantly when we are seeing very creative patients. Often early in therapy, creative patients will analyze and examine not only the therapist but family and friends of the patient in a way that usurps the role of the therapist. This is certainly normal and can later be used by interpreting the feelings of competition that the patient is having. It is important for the therapist to not respond with his or her own needs to make the statement that "I am an expert in this area, and I am as creative and interesting as you are."

Another problem for the therapist is one's own bias about highly charged issues such as the theoretical structure or underpinnings of one's own therapeutic technique. After all, the therapeutic technique the therapist uses and all the theory that goes along with it is helpful in forming an hypothesis. However, this should not hinder the therapist from "going with the patient," if the patient's material must be forced into a model that does not fit the patient's needs. If this becomes an issue, it is important to review the patient and the psychotherapy approach being used with another psychotherapist. The use of a "peer group" to study these issues is extremely helpful. This will often tease out a bias in therapy that is detrimental to the progress of the patient and will encourage a more creative approach by the psychotherapist.

Another problem for the therapist may be overidentification. It is important that the therapist maintain a certain amount of objectivity in observing the patient's interactions with the psychotherapist. Care must be taken not to get "sucked into" the patient's very rich and creative style and thought processes. It is important not to reinforce neurotic or narrowing defenses, which may actually produce a decrease in creative productivity.

A final problem for the therapist is that one must remain authentic or natural whenever possible. This allows for not only longer professional life, minimizing "burnout" but also provides a more consistent figure in therapy for the patient. The therapist who remains natural and responsive to patients will find them increasingly risk-taking and able to explore their own outer boundaries, as they are sure of the consistency and firmness of the therapist's own personality structure.

In summary, then, the creative person is one of the great joys of our world and can be a stimulating challenge in psychotherapy. Psychotherapists must confirm the authenticity of the patient's creative impulses. They can also help to remove roadblocks to the creative person's creativity with the techniques of psychotherapy. In this manner, the patient will grow and so will the psychotherapist.

REFERENCES

Arieti, S. (1976). *Creativity*. New York: Basic Books.

Barron, F. (1963). *Creativity and psychological health*. NY: Van Nostrand.

Dellas, M., & Faier, E.L. (1970). Identification of creativity: The individual. *Psychological Bulletin, 73*, 55-73.

Freud, S. (1963). The paths to the formation of symptoms. In J. Strachey (Ed. and Trans.), *The standard edition of the complete psychological works of Sigmund Freud* (Vol. 16, pp. 358-377). London: Hogarth Press. (Original work published 1917).

Hutzler, J.C., & Pinta, E. (1977). The false acknowledgment phenomenon in psychotherapy. *American Journal of Psychoanalysis, 37*, 167-170.

Kris, E. (1952). *Psychoanalytic explorations in art*. New York: International Universities Press.

Kubie, L.S. (1958). *Neurotic distortion of the creative process*. KS: University of Kansas Press.

Schubert, D.S.P. (1973). Intelligence as necessary but not sufficient for creativity. *Journal of Genetic Psychology, 122*, 45-47.

Schubert, D.S.P. (in press). Creativity and the ability to cope. In F. Flach (Ed.), *The creative mind*. Buffalo, NY: Bearly Press.

Stein, M.I. (in press). Book chapter in F. Flach (Ed.), *The creative mind*. Buffalo, NY: Bearly Press.

Storr, A. (in press). Book chapter in F. Flach (Ed.), *The creative mind*. Buffalo, NY: Bearly Press.

Creative Patience

Sarah Zaraleya-Harari

SUMMARY. In a combination of playfulness and seriousness, this article reveals a therapist's working secret about how she sees her patients' psychotherapeutic processes enhanced when selectively and creatively woven into and extending the themes of her own life process. Descriptions are given of the therapist's creativity in developing a semester framework for psychotherapy and a method, theory, and technique related to the use of psychic energy, with graphic illustrations and examples that include unconventional work with a creative artist, the use of playfulness and imagination in individual and group psychotherapy and its rippling effects.

"It's like trying to show a fish that it's swimming in water," exclaimed Ken Fisher in his frustration with a patient one day.

The topic was creativity and I was the patient.

When I courageously admitted to friend and teacher, Bud (Bernard) Fisher, that I kept seeing aspects of my own problems in the analyses of patients' projective protocols, he said, "That is what most of us do without admitting it."

My longtime friend, English Professor Blossom Feinstein's largest contribution to my life is the theme of her six-hundred-page doctoral dissertation on creativity as making order out of chaos.

Presently, I am not working with Fishermen, rather with a Fox (Warren), and I find that there are major themes that have meaning in different ways and degrees for most people. When they are true for the therapist, they can possibly be more true for the patient. When patients are working in their depths, struggling with some-

Sarah Zaraleya-Harari, EdD 1969, Yeshiva University, is a school psychologist and in private practice in New City. She is editor of the bulletin of the Rockland Center for the Arts, on the staff of Nyack Hospital, and a codirector of the Humanistic Psychology Center of New York. Mailing address: 10 Wyndham Lane, New City, NY 10956.

thing, that is when they can be most creative. And if I can connect with them at that level, there is a treasured synchronicity in the therapeutic process.

For the ken of Fisher, the wisdom of Fox, and the bud to blossom, I had to let go of my fears of admitting what I do, in order to do what I do.

I hope I will be not marked sternly for adding myself to the roster of creative patients.

My creative bent showed itself in how I began my practice in 1969 (Strear, 1971, 1972; Zaraleya, 1979). Working in my living room, I did therapy on a semester basis, charging in advance for five months and seeing people when and for as long as necessary. Appointments however could not be made in advance . . . only at the time the necessity arose. The system worked beautifully with the average session lasting for one hour and average attendance about one in ten days. Phone calls at any time and regular weekly group therapy sessions were part of our contracts.

At the end of Joan's first therapy session I was sure that she would step right out into traffic and get herself killed. She was so oblivious to what was going on around her, and so depressed, that I insisted we call a relative to come for her. At that time I was working in my own apartment and I had to lock my two cats in the bedroom before Joan would come in. A few years later, when I moved to live and work in a setting which was a combination office, school, and home; and in which Joan found herself having to walk through a waiting room, which had a secretary typing and answering the phone, she did not like that. She also didn't like the vibrations in the new apartment, which I didn't like either.

Joan said that she had contracted with me to have therapy in a home-like setting where there was good energy. I agreed with her and I rented space in a quiet apartment several blocks away. She insisted upon paying one-half the fee for the space.

Joan is a painter and she used to bring her paintings and talk about them in relation to her therapy and her problems, bringing her parts into harmony. She actually experienced herself in five parts: wife, maid, whore, lady, and painter who conversed with each other at home. Only one at a time came to a therapy session. We kept a special nail in the wall for her to hang her paintings in my apartment and later in the room that I rented.

In the course of therapy, her paintings improved considerably and she became part of a group that had annual exhibits. After she sold several paintings, Joan rented a loft near her home, in which to paint more seriously. She went through all the problems related to independence and its effect on her marriage. In time, Joan was not as cautious about my tucking the cats away. She had done some secretarial work for me when the cats were around and had gotten used to them. Joan would say that these were the *only* cats that she could be with. Later the cats were no problem and no issue at all. Joan talked about whether to have a child. She wanted one very much, but occasionally would think that she and her husband perhaps were not the kind of people who ought to bring a child into the world. Joan vacillated in relation to this and finally decided to hold off. She did get herself a kitten and she would talk about that kitten in the fashion of a true cat lover.

Joan and I had an appointment for a therapy session at six p.m. one evening. Through some confusion, I was late for the appointment. By the time I taxied there she had left. I felt very bad. She lived an hour's drive away. When I got back to my apartment and called her, the first thing she said was, "I'm very angry and I don't think I'll be coming to therapy any more." I invited her to talk about what happened. She said, "Well, when people want something special, as I did in having you meet me in a special place, I have to expect that things aren't going to work out the way they do for people who go along with the conventional way of doing things. I came to talk to you about things that were on my mind. Yes, I can express my anger, but I don't want to spend my energy and my money expressing my anger to you. I think what I'm going to do is find another therapist who is near me and who won't be putting themselves out as much as you have to; who won't be disrupting their normal routine. . . . Three years ago, I was crazy and I had to see you. Now I'm not jumping out of windows or off bridges. Now I'm not considering that or threatening it and I don't have to see you." She talked for a little while about one or two of the things that had been on her mind and we did make another appointment. There was a great deal of anger wanting an outlet. But the major points she made were that she didn't have to see me, that she was responsible for setting up a situation in which she might not get what she wanted every time, that she could do something to change that, that she was angry and able to express it clearly and appropriately, that she was no longer crazy and she could make the decision herself as to whom she would see and make it more convenient for herself. This was the beginning of the end and we terminated therapy a few months later.

This all happened about eight years ago. Joan calls me at least once a year on my birthday, and sends photos of her now six-year-old daughter along with some of her drawings.

In reviewing the process of our therapy, there appear to be a number of fairly unconventional aspects: that is, Joan's doing secretarial work in my home, our semester contract, my respecting her sensitivity to unpleasant vibrations, renting space to accommodate Joan's reasonable request, allowing her to share in the expense, cats roaming around, a special nail for her paintings and using them in the therapy.

These aspects of our work together which describe a unique relationship had at least as much to do with Joan's emotional growth and the strengthening of her sense of self as the more conventional working through of problem themes in the therapy session.

It is only after I do what I do that I know what I did. (If I know it then.) The most difficult aspect is the acceptance that we are part of a larger process.

* * *

I have enjoyed working with many young people who came to New York to study and to find work in one of the art media, including painting, photography, acting, and operatic singing. Through attending rehearsals, shows, performances, and parties in their honor, I have become involved in their lives more than I have with other patients, sometimes continuing by the exchange of letters and gifts, connections for many years after the completion of therapy. One former patient "keeps my identity hidden inside her daughter SuZanne's name."

From the time I wrote my first love poem at the age of seven, I have been involved with writing or painting in some form. Most recently I painted on large canvases the designs that illustrate the Zaraleya Psychoenergetic Technique, which includes the use of art therapy.

I have developed a theory, method, and technique (Zaraleya, 1980, 1982) which I use with my patients. In its use, we consider ourselves fitting a concept of energy, existing in time and space, past, present, and future and representing the basic material of which the Universe and everything in it is derived, and as such, aim to direct that energy of which we are made constructively, positively, and wholesomely. Rather than consider how we use our time, we consider how we use our energy.

Proposed within this system, there are four major phases of energy usage. (see Figure I). Briefly, they are:

I. *Intra-activity* — representing the use of energy related to the inner self, as in meditation;
II. *Interactivity* — representing the interchange of energy with the outer world of people, things, places, and ideas;
III. *Synergy* — representing the integration of new energies with former energies; and
IV. *Transformation* — the energy phase requiring recognition and acknowledgment of the experiences of phases I, II, and III; and then changing our thinking, feeling, and behavior and how we use our energy to be in keeping with what we have been through. It requires that we behave in ways true to our inner being, reflecting our life experiences. That would have us continuously growing and changing, in the reality of ordinary existence.

Different people spend their energies more in quiet meditative states, others use their energies in great amounts of outer activities. I have found that creative people are more apt to make connections between their inner goings-on and the happenings or occurrences in the outer world (Phase III — Synergy).

Their creative blocks usually represent difficulties in how they use their energy. We look to the Energy Dynamics records we keep during their sessions for ways they use their energy — destructively or negatively, and the ways they would like to use their energy — constructively or positively. Changing those behaviors requiring the redirection of energy is extremely difficult, calling for considerable courage on their parts and encouragement from me and, where applicable, from fellow group-therapy patients.

I find I have to move in and out of a fairly strict psychoanalytically oriented psychotherapy and a very real direct personal relationship. We laugh together and sometimes cry together. Humor, playfulness, and fun are very important in binding and connecting people as well as in increasing positive synergic energy, good health, and good living.

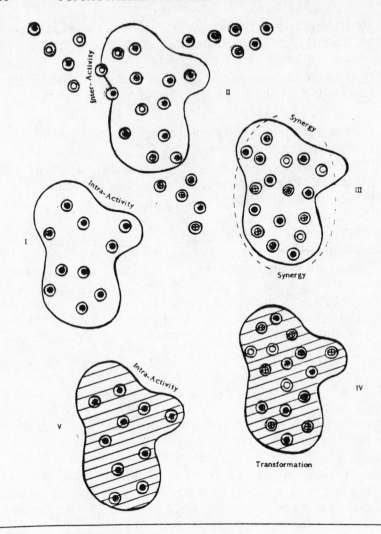

A black and white rendition of the five colored Charts of the Zaraleya Psychoenergetic Technique illustrate the containment, exchange and integration of psychic energy, the Transformation of the energy constellation and the beginning of its next cycle.

FIGURE 1

One day as I was sitting with Jane Ellen in a therapy session, I suddenly had an image of standing on the couch and continuing the session in that position. I decided to do it. She said "Is this what we are supposed to do now?" and stood up on her couch too. At first we laughed; then we became serious. It seemed important and challenging to her to express what she had to say in this unusual position. In the group session that followed, Jane Ellen announced that she had spent part of her session standing on the couch, and in short order they were all up there fooling around and laughing and holding on to each other as they switched places. I think it was especially helpful to those of us more fearful of our irrational selves.

This experience had a further ripple effect. Jane Ellen began to use humor to generate energy in the form of enthusiasm, in teaching her below-level junior high school English class. The following is a great limerick written by one of her students:

> May I have some cream cheese — to go on my bagel please!
> If I eat it plain,
> I will go insane —
> I'm begging on bended knees.

Recently, Madelaine, an actress who had been through a particularly painful year, reminded me that in her third session, when she complained that she was still having anxiety attacks, I said, "You've had three lessons and you want to play a sonata?" She values the humor in our sessions, and its healing effect.

One weekend when Gloria, an opera star, was anxious about being alone, she helped herself turn that painful energy to constructive use by crocheting a bright and colorful shawl from leftover scraps of wool. It will always remain a personal memento of her courage.

Investigating how he used his energy, and given the opportunity to look at his life differently, Fred, a chiropractor, reports:

> I feel OK while I'm here with you . . . but I have much self-doubt at midnight. Actually, I never experienced self-doubt like that before. I feel good about that. I am making an incredible effort to rearrange the world to do what I want it to do.
>
> I am thirty-eight years old and my eyes are open. It is possible to make decisions. I come first. I feel tense and nervous and upset. But that's fine. I like it.
>
> Nobody ever told me that I was responsible for how my life goes. It never crossed my mind. Life just moved along for me. I used to just let circumstances take me from one thing to another. That it's possible to direct your own life energy is a novel idea, and when I tried, it worked.

Some creative patients have a meaningful form to use in which to express themselves and their conscious and unconscious quest. In this process often they are carried to deeper and wider dimensions of consciousness. They may come into therapy with more familiarity with the territory, so to speak, and soon become actively involved in using the therapy itself as an art form.

I include under the heading of creative patients some people who are not creative artists in the usual sense but whose approach to their work as teachers, veterinarians, stewardesses, or sales people is as it would be toward an art form.

Characteristics of creative patients may include the tendency to test the limits of the boundaries set for them. This may be reflected in such behaviors as coming to their sessions late, having an alcoholic drink directly before their session, missing payments, missing sessions, flattering the therapist, walking in as if modeling their clothing outfits, wearing unusual or scanty clothing and sitting nonchalantly with their private parts nearly exposed.

Other characteristics of creative patients may include their willingness to experience the new, different, and inventive. This may be seen in their eagerness to learn to try things out, to see from a new or different perspective. I even have been able to direct such patients to dream.

They seem to want challenge. They are usually most responsive to appreciation, support, and encouragement. They respond to visual representations of themselves working on their own lives that I sometimes sketch.

For example, I draw two round circles to show two whole people and how they may remain self-contained while interacting with each other, each retaining its whole self to return to, no matter how intimate they may be together (see Figure II, Representation A).[1]

Then I draw a Yin and Yang symbol separated into two parts to describe two separate people, who rather than seek to fulfill themselves look to or for someone else, either to fill or be filled by, in order to become whole (see Figure II, Representation B).[1]

These graphic representations of both the need and the fear of separateness and intimacy can have a strong impact and can be helpful to those who visualize ideas.

Also usually characteristic of creative patients is their ability to experience largely and beyond the superficial, and their respect for irrational experiences including thoughts that seem irrelevant and farfetched, as well as feelings, hunches, and sensory awareness. I

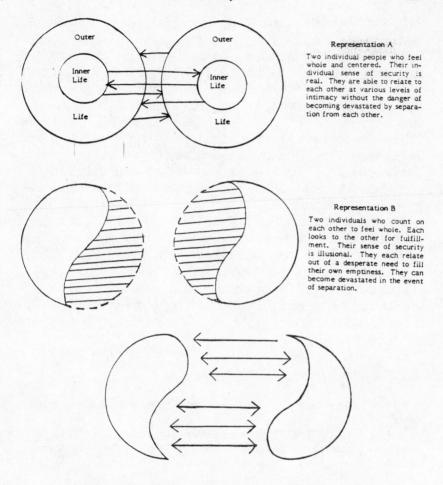

Representation A

Two individual people who feel whole and centered. Their individual sense of security is real. They are able to relate to each other at various levels of intimacy without the danger of becoming devastated by separation from each other.

Representation B

Two individuals who count on each other to feel whole. Each looks to the other for fulfillment. Their sense of security is illusional. They each relate out of a desperate need to fill their own emptiness. They can become devastated in the event of separation.

We all are interdependent on each other. However, to the degree that our dependence on others interferes with our own personal growth and development, does our relationship with those others deteriorate.

Two people seeking fulfillment by connecting with another in place of being and becoming whole unto themselves are drawn together like magnets.

Since it is impossible realistically to fulfill oneself in this manner, the expectations are not met and eventually the relationship can become a terrible disappointment.

FIGURE II

learned from one patient to experience the presence of what she called fairies. They appear in the form of a tiny flash of light, like a lightning bug.

For those in the arts, the need for structure in the therapy situation corresponds to the framework of limitation they are used to in their own work and within which they then have the freedom of fullest expression.

Their need for the therapist to be equally creative and encouraging corresponds to the guidance and alternate possibilities offered by the director or editor; and their need for appreciation, support, and encouragement corresponds to their audiences and their followings.

Incidentally, I have found that though therapy may help solve problems that formerly may have stimulated the work of some creative patients, it also opens up to them "a most beautiful payoff of heretofore unknown previously unrecognized, and as-yet-unsolved problems" (Fuller, 1975).[2]

The plan and the quest are different. We do all we can, including not doing; and we have to allow as well for the process, about which we may have no conscious knowledge.

The quest is revealed as the plan is carried out.

For example, while busy working on the subject of this paper, something of a larger quality emerged — both this concept and its name, Creative Patience.

NOTES

1. These representations are part of a manuscript of an unpublished book by the author.
2. R. Buckminster Fuller made this statement in relation to his lifelong geometrical and philosophical explorations. One of his "most exciting discoveries is that local discovery leads to a complex of further discoveries."

REFERENCES

Fuller, B.R. (1975). *Synergetics, Explorations in the geometry of thinking.* New York: Macmillan.

Strear, S. (1971). A new approach. *The Journal of Clinical Issues in Psychology, 2*(2), 18-19.

Zaraleya, S. (1979). How do you pay me? Let me count the ways. *VOICES: The Art and Science of Psychotherapy, 14*(4), 44-47.

Zaraleya, S. (1980). Zaraleya psychoenergetic technique. In R. Herink (Ed.), *The psychotherapy handbook* (pp. 705-710). New York: New American Library.

Zaraleya, S. (1982). Zaraleya psychoenergetic technique. In J. Hariman (Ed.), *Compendium of Major Psychotherapeutic Methods* (pp. 330-338). Springfield, MA: Charles C Thomas.

The Creative Patient:
The Use of Poetry
in Psychotherapy

SUMMARY. This article deals with the dynamics of poetry as an effective ancillary tool in clinical practice in dealing with individuals psychologically. In the hands of the professional clinician, poetry may be used efficaciously as a sharp, probing psychodiagnostic tool to assess patient malfunctioning, personality evaluation, and behavioral manifestations. Poetry therapy delineates the awareness of underlying tension and anxiety, and offers psychological release to hasten the healing process toward greater overall maturity, by revealing the individuality of the person. As a therapeutic process it helps the psychologist to recognize in the patient those attributes within the self that form the personality in action.

The service function of poetry in a therapeutic format is stressed, with poetry utilized well in relation to sociological functioning of the individual as a distinct aspect of educational, psychological, and habilitation programs. The article considers background material and conceptualizations from the fields of behavioral sciences, literature, philosophy, and the discipline of psychological services.

In recent years, research has indicated that therapists in psychology, psychiatry, mental health areas, and behavioral sciences have come to recognize poetry as an extremely powerful, though subtle, healing instrument in reaching troubled minds, and stirring up, freeing, and calming the inner feelings of mentally ill individuals. Poetry illuminates the darkest recesses of the mind, with a power to make the individual happier and more fulfilled. Poetry has also

Hirsch Lazaar Silverman, PhD, Licensed Psychologist, ABPP, is a Diplomate in Clinical, Family, and Forensic Psychology, and Fellow of the American Psychological Association. He is Professor Emeritus, Graduate Division, Seton Hall University. Mailing address: 123 Gregory Ave., West Orange, NJ 07052.

been useful in helping the sociopathic or psychopathological person find new and better ways of dealing with life.

For poetry as a therapeutic process is one of the natural human resources for healing. Psychologically, poetry can be a creative clinical and therapeutic healing force when it gives one a new way of life; for the troubled child or youth sings a song that is characteristic of his or her troubles. One sings the same song, in fact, to all of life's experiences; and, although one sings as one lives, there is increasing research evidence that one may live as one sings and live in a new way if one "sings" a new song.

It is the thesis of the author, then, that poetry therapy is an opportunity scientifically, a tool, for psychotherapists to share with other human beings as a manner of creative endeavor through which they make use of the self in the therapeutic relationship, especially in dealing with dependency, anger, sexuality, personality factors, and family relationships.

I

Poetry therapy as related to psychotherapy is a form of treatment for problems of emotional nature in which a trained clinician deliberately establishes a professional relationship with a patient through the use of poetry with the object of removing, modifying, or retarding existing symptoms; of mediating disturbed patterns of behavior; and of promoting positive personality growth and development. Personality growth takes into consideration the aspect of personality maturation in order to assist the individual in achieving a more gratifying relationship with people in one's environments.

The truly basic elements in a sound poetry therapy session are *unity* and *simplicity*. Small problems are necessarily more easily solved than larger ones, but at the same time the gestalt, the pattern of the whole, must be kept in mind. The center of the answer to a question should be the point of the question, and the circumference no wider than is needed to answer the question adequately at the time. *After all, dialogue is seeking truth.*

In therapy, the search involves having willingness of mind to reach out to that which is not yet fully understood, or even to something which at first perhaps repels the individual. When one idea supplements another, as in professional therapy, often a joint truth emerges from the dialogue of persons who started even with divergent beliefs.

Therapists should realize that *poetry is a representation of an idea*. Contents and character in poetry are idealized, and this idealization bears a high consistency with individualization. Poetry is indicative of the originality of grace, refinement, purity, and good feeling; the poet exhibiting correct moral perception in his lines. It is, in essence, originality energizing in the world of beauty. All of this may be effectively utilized in poetry therapy. An immortal instinct, deep within the spirit of man, is a sense of the beautiful. It is no mere appreciation of the beauty before us, but an effort to reach the beauty above. *Life is essentially beautiful, and life is the poet's glossary, not literature. The poets in general love the beauty of the fact, and tell the actual and factual truth, with a belief in realism.*

Poetry in therapy can be a treatise of existence, for most poets talk sincerely about the simple things, as well as about the sophisticated ones — those that too often are forgotten in living; and such thoughts are neither deified nor sentimentalized. Thus, when by poetry we find ourselves melted to tears, we weep then not through excess of pleasure, but through a certain petulant, impatient sorrow at our inability to grasp now, wholly, here on earth, at once and forever, those divine and rapturous joys of which through the poem we attain to but brief and indeterminate glimpses. The implications of poetry therapy are patent.

II

For some years, the author has used poetry therapy in clinical practice. For poetry has healing properties, and reaches in diverse ways the behavioral and emotional problems in many types of people; and it makes for changes in them, illuminating the darkest recesses of the mind, with a power to make the person happier, more fulfilled.

Poetry therapy emphasizes in its approach and procedure the relation of the poetic experience to mental health as a distinct aspect of psychological, educational, and habilitation programs, with the specific use of poetry as a valid tool in dealing with psychological problems creatively. Poetry therapy attempts to delineate creatively the awareness of underlying tension and anxiety, and thus offers psychological release to hasten the healing process toward greater overall maturity by revealing more succinctly the individuality of the patient. This therapeutic process also helps the psychologist-

therapist to recognize in the patient those attributes within the self
that form the personality in action.

An awareness of one's self in terms of needs and the ways one
seeks to fulfill one's needs are essential to the poetry therapist as is
the awareness of his or her social role, with all its expectations. One
must understand one's own set of values and beliefs and know how
these may enter into one's perceptions of clients and of the situations in which they find themselves. A great deal of knowledge of
self is the prerequisite for the therapist's wise use of himself or
herself. And knowledge of self exists only where there is a sense of
acceptance and comfort with one's self.

The therapist of necessity is a person of integrity and maturity; to
the extent that these are lacking, there will be flaws in one's therapeutic relationships. The most important aspect of poetry therapy in
terms of mental health is the degree of quality of communication
that takes place. Communication not only reveals the patient's
problems and feelings but provides the clues to the therapist's feelings; it is the way in which the therapist in turn makes himself or
herself known to clients. In fine, it is the way in which the therapist
takes the client "unto himself or herself."

Professional dialogue in therapy includes conversation and discussion with a purpose, with poetry used as a means. It is reason's
only real weapon. It is a civilized procedure and operation, demo-
cratic and constructive. To take useful part in making decisions is to
seek understanding through consideration of alternatives, and
through it individuals attain insight and understanding. Such dialogue requires common substance, and certainly requires a large
measure of goodwill. It begins in an act of faith, the assumption that
those who are in therapy will speak in honesty for the purpose of
reaching understanding, and with balanced generosity. It is by comparison of views that we reason our way toward truth. We increase
the odds of finding the best and most feasible solution to problems
by considering alternatives, psychologically.

III

In and through the creativity inherent in poetry, hopefully as we
individuals may reach maturity—the reaching in time of that sta-
tionary stage in our individuality where no further change need take
place, to be sure of a kind of fixity in our individual lives. Yet, in
truth, poetry teaches us that in the properly mature person no articu-

lation, no thought, no faculty is ever so utterly excluded to the person, directly or indirectly. For maturity actually is the human capacity on an individual basis to evaluate and delineate situations and experiences into singularities, parts, or sections; and then to reform them into a gestalt, or pattern, a configuration most efficacious to immediate needs and circumstances.

Poetry therapists must believe implicitly in life, in its manifestations, grasping existence as a whole. A large naturalism, with vigor, with certain idealistic generalizations, with a gentle radicalism, with a calm and cultured honesty—with these, therapists today ought to concern themselves. Conscious—almost self-conscious—philosophizing, mixed with thoughts that are both strong and delicate, causes the therapist to analyze poetry as an art, and its object; pleasurable appreciation. Poetry exists for its own sake; it is a world, in a restricted sense, of its own. It should serve as an end but can be used therapeutically as a means. In each poem can be found a great spirit, a profound experience; disclosed, it suffices. The therapist's mind ought to be nourished by liberal studies; and from those studies one should extract the kernel of substance for one's poetry therapy, not contenting oneself with the husk of accident. The therapist's aim should be clarity, as opposed to contemporary obscurantist tendencies, and, in the manner of style, purity and freedom from mannerism, as distinct from the contemporary tendency to substitute mannerism for true originality in the therapeutic process. The therapist at all events must base his or her convictions upon inquiry and meditation; these should not merely be the mere rags and shreds of others' thought.

Recognizing the ambrosia that nourishes the soul in everything around him or her, the therapist perceives it also in the suggestive ideas that come through poetry. However, it is to be recognized that poetry does not abound in devastating opinionativeness; mystical obfuscation is avoided; and lines of poetry should not be interpreted as based on verbal inconsequentialities. While the poet's range may not be all-inclusive, his or her material is not dependent on time. Poetry achieves permanence only when the medium is not words but *elements*. This, too, the therapist must recognize; for although his or her appeal is human, the poet has convictions rather than sentiment alone: convictions of a philosophy that may disturb readers, of searching truth rather than of sweet truisms. The therapist using poetry as a technique must therefore be no less discriminatingly realistic.

IV

To be sure, poetry therapy cannot be used effectively with all patients; but the individual with better than average educational background is a prime candidate for such effort. He or she can find through the uses of poetry therapy many means of outlet, of expression, of meaningful expression.

The healing effect is more likely to happen in the writing of poetry when the writing is *spontaneous*. A person can sit down and write out a strong feeling of some kind, and out of the writing will emerge rhythms of sounds — especially if one bears in mind that essentially one is writing poetry. By sensibly telling oneself one is writing a poem one is opening the door to freedom of expression. One is saying that one does not have to make anyone understand one and that one does not have to address anyone in particular. One is saying that fiction and fact may be interwoven, and not in conflict. One is free to play with words and images: to turn them, twist them, scramble them, listen to them, and look at them.

For poetry is a kind of spontaneous experience. In school we were trained to write a poem of a certain meter and a certain rhyme, and we struggled to find words that fit the pattern. The whole experience was frustrating rather than healing. The therapist discovers a new aspect of the healing power of poetry through spontaneous writing. One aspect of such an approach to poetry is that a poem is *not* evaluated in terms of literary, moral, and esthetics values; or in terms of whether anyone likes, or dislikes, the poem.

This degree of freedom for spontaneous expression is helpful to the healing effect psychologically. On the other hand, the attention to the devices of sight and sound contributes to the training of poets but not necessarily to healing — although the awareness of sights and sounds is part of a healthy outreach to the world around us. The form and structure of poetry are not discarded in spontaneous writing but are allowed to merge from spontaneous writing.

The *reading* of poems as well as the *writing* of poems is a healing force in poetry therapy. Three conditions seem to promote healing through the reading of poems. *One* is that the poem be read word for word, in order that the rhythm and rhyme, the assonance and alliteration of the poem may be appreciated. (If one skims through a poem, these qualities are lost.) A *second* condition is that the poem must be heard. One may listen to another person read a poem, one may read it aloud to oneself, or one may "hear" it in one's mind as one reads it silently. The *third* condition for healing is what may be called the *iso-principle*, which means that the feeling of the poem must be the same as the feeling of the person hearing the poem. If one were not responding to a certain poem, one might do well to discontinue that poem and thumb through the pages for another poem or another poet, as if looking over a bill of fare for something appealing or satisfying. (But, it should be pointed out, mere poetry by itself is not always a therapeutic force. If one feels in despair and reads a despairing poem that has no underlying hope, one could spiral downward in one's feelings. If one feels too much despair, one may even stop reading before arriving at the more hopeful portions of the poem.)

With an impulse themselves to create, poetry therapists find a continually fresh delight in the variety and wonder of life. Therapists should try to make poems radiate a new spirit, free in expression, unhampered in choice of subject, keen in psychology and philosophy. Therapists should strive to use poetry with deep notes and large themes. Poetry, the art of solitude, requires a great deal of thought, a great deal of silent work, and all the sincerity of which an individual's nature is capable. For the poet, more existence oftentimes is glorious. Life, while coarse and difficult and frequently dangerous and dirty, is not for the poet splendid at the heart. The poet's work shares the fears, hopes, angers, and struggles of the prosaic world. The therapist rightly explains these facts to clients and relates them, involvedly, to individuals he works with professionally.

The therapeutic effort must explore present difficulties and their influence on a person's conflict. The therapist clarifies problems and makes suggestions for possible solutions. There is an effort to untangle the character distortion, to let the patient gain inner strength and the ability to choose the direction of his or her contact with people. The poetry therapist has a definite task and goal. One does not stop at suggestion but tries to help the patient achieve deeper characterological changes. It is significant that in the therapeutic technique the need for conformity is often emphasized so much. Integration into the community is no less a real psychotherapeutic goal.

The peculiar functions of poetry for the therapist are twofold: to transfuse emotion and to transmit thought. The thought should dominate the words; the poet hopefully had sought for depths rather than surfaces. In poetry, if it is to be vital and dynamic, there must be a fusing of mood, accent, and image in a fresh intensity. Poetry is, as a totality, an artlessness that is more than an art. The province of poetry is the entire range of human experience and that vast area of moral destiny.

Therapeutically, poetry should represent something more than verbal jugglery; it should stand for art in a larger sense, and should embody the features of a personality rather than the dexterities of rhetorical craftsmanship. The poet's lines somehow help to turn on the counselee's quest for absolute reality and to an affirmation of human values. Poets occupy themselves with the themes of life and death, which for the patients may sharpen some aspects of their living: beauty, love, quiet days of thought. This may develop a new awareness in feeling.

V

Truth is unquestionably one of the purest and truest of all poetical themes, and through truth in poetry patients are led to perceive a harmony where none was apparent before. In therapy, there is an increasing concern with the present; in the past, to be sure, there has been too much dehumanized mysticism in poetry. For poets embrace a different consciousness and a greater awareness of life; and the therapist should capitalize on it. A return of actuality, poetry reveals a deep and philosophical nature expressing itself in terms of high seriousness, which again constitutes a therapeutic aspect.

The therapist using poetry as an art and as a technique should be endowed with a critical mind. The mind of the therapist cannot withdraw from the spontaneous expression of insight and imagination to a minute diligence in the mere formation of lines. Then it is that poetry will gain both in intensity and in sincerity for the counselee. Also, the poetry therapist should strive for originality. An art of emotional expression, poetry, in its psychological and philosophical sense, is not what remains at a level: it is the exceptional, the extraordinary, the powerful, the unexpected, that soars far above the general trend. poetry means the power to move people's hearts and minds.

The purpose of poetry therapy is to help a maladjusted person to learn, by various ways and in time, new ways of dealing with thinking about oneself and other people, and new responses to one's life situations. The methods employed by therapists to achieve this end are varied, but the basis underlying the differing approaches is primarily to teach patients to develop more constructive concepts of themselves. The poetry therapist must come to realize that a person with difficulties is the product *of* the causes of those difficulties: so often environmental, patterns of living, circumstantial, and interpersonal relationships.

Poetry therapy in this sense, then, should be looked upon—by both the patient and the therapist—as repair work on a professional basis of science and art, and not as a complete rebirth of the personality. For the results of therapy are necessarily limited by such factors as the caliber of the original material, as well as by the individual (constitution plus young ego), the degree of damage (infantile traumata and adult frustrations), and what remains to be worked with (adult ego plus the reality situation).

Again, the implications for poetry therapy are wide and broad and deep. By implication, poetry therapy may well be the treatment of mental disorders by the use of suggestion, counseling, persuasion, advising, direction, and the like, with the purpose or goal of relieving the patient of distressing neurotic symptoms or discordant personality characteristics that interfere with satisfactory adaptation to a world of people and events. (Perhaps it is not so much *how* therapy is *done*, but how *effective* it is professionally and scientifically that is the ultimate criterion of therapy.)

Whatever our eventual differential definition of poetry therapy, it would benefit our profession of psychology to frame it within the general guidelines of the reflective, creative psychologist model in the light no less of a coming-of-age rallying point for guiding our specialty as a tool past mere technocracy and toward responsible, integrated science-art, and service.

In a sense, poetry therapy creeps into the person's psyche as silent as a bruise, to make the individual happy and better adjusted, to feel better, do better, be better, through self-search. Shelly saw poetry as "the very image of life expressed in its eternal truth." Poetry attracts the intellect and has in itself beauty pleasing to the moral nature. It tends to be idealistic as well as individualistic. The originality found in poems has to do with the power of abstraction for one's self.

VI

As regards the domain of psychological therapy, the therapist should have a great deal of self-knowledge, particularly in terms of personal needs and the ways to fulfill those needs; and he or she must strive for a two-way communication with clients. Therapy should be involved with reducing the anxiety and hostility that come from a stress-filled world. Human beings have a need to survive and want order, intimacy, uniqueness, and productivity. Karen Horney (1937) observed that character drives in three lines: toward, against, and away from people. While one of these lines will be prominent, what causes pain in the person is the anxiety caused by conflict within these lines. The poetry therapist, in trying to relieve the individual's suffering, attempts to untangle the individual's character distortion.

Poetry, then, can be used as a means of communication between therapist and client as part of the professional dialogue. The poetry would be the common ground in a dialogue that searches for alternatives to solving conflicts. This does not mean that there is constant talking. The importance of *thoughtful silence* that can occur naturally in the consideration of the poem's truth must be recognized. The poetry that is selected should be attractive to the self of both the therapist and client. The therapist should look for works, as already indicated, that transfuse emotion and transmit thought. Features of personality rather than mere rhetoric are emphasized. Themes that help the counselee's search for reality and will serve to reaffirm human values are most desirable. One should use poetry as a technique and as an art for the pleasurable appreciation that can be derived. Clarity, as well as a realistic approach, should be a major aim.

The more we know about interpersonal, intrapsychic, body, energy, and transpersonal phenomena, the more their underlying principles converge in and through poetry therapy. Concepts such as truth and choice are ubiquitous, and it appears that perhaps there is only one fear, one teaching, one cause of disease, one social problem, and one marital difficulty: the lack of true poetic and spiritual insight in human beings.

All creatures value life. Valuing is a process we will use until we die. We re-create it anew with every piece of new data or new living. We need to work on the processes of values clarification. Holistic education in a poetic setting develops mind, body, emotions, imagination, intuition, and spirit. As therapists we must explore the development and integration of each of these functions through self-concept development, sensory awareness, psychocalisthenics, gestalt awareness, guided fantasy, psychosynthesis, affirmation, and basic thinking as individuals.

There seems to be a yearning among many of today's young people to reach back into the world of yesterday. Yet old and young live separately, feel alienated. Through poetry there is a meeting of minds, an examination of the stories each was told that set them on separate pathways. Through group experiences in poetry reading and writing, we find places where our journeys can meet to enrich each other's lives.

Actualizing therapy in a creative manner through poetry espouses a core wherein the polarities of feeling are synthesized into an entity. It is a unique and individual core which distinguishes man from all other beings. Its existence is demonstrated by a series of experimental exercises involving the mind and its relationship to thinking and feeling in poetic expression.

As time passes through days and into years, its passage of course brings movement and change. Though clocks record the hours, it is the experiencing of change by the living person, that is, phenomenal time, which is the focus of our lives. The time/person interface must be examined from several perspectives, including conceptualized dimensions of change, duration of positive experiences, membership in long-term groups, and functioning of healthy personalities over time. Poetry therapy serves this role effectively.

Poetry, through a competent therapist, provides solace to the troubled mind while it gives utterance to inward emotions. Poetry therapy is seen as repair work done by the combination of science and art. The poetry therapist must ultimately come to realize that a person with difficulties is the product of the causes of those difficulties. It also should be remembered that the results of therapy may be limited to such things as the quality of various relevant factors: the individual, the scope of the damage, and what is left of the person; and, certainly, poetry therapy can and should be used in conjunction with other methods.

As an art and a science in combination, poetry therapy truly is a discipline. The therapeutic process in poetry involves the interpretation of not merely words semantically, but the deeper meanings, the mood elements, the very substance of thought. While all literary forms are essentially major forms of creativity, poetry lends itself more poignantly to the healing process. For poetry in psychotherapeutic intervention discloses more clearly the relation between and among processes of the individual's mentality, personality, and mental health functioning.

REFERENCE

Horney, K. (1937). *Neurotic personality of our times*. New York: Norton.

Poetry and Prose —
Experiencing the Creative Patient

Alexander Jasnow

SUMMARY. After a brief discussion of the attribute of creativity as it is perceived in Western culture today, this attribute is further explored in a patient population. A comparison was made between two groupings, one of "creative" patients and the other of relatively "uncreative" patients. An initial cursory examination did not reveal any marked clinical differences between these two groups. What did stand out, however, was the therapist's experiential reaction to the individuals in the two groups. The "creative" patients were experienced as retaining to a greater degree than the others a capacity for "play." The therapeutic implications of this finding are further explored.

"The rich are different" wrote F. Scott Fitzgerald in the opening lines of "The Rich Boy." It is tempting to ride on his coattails and simply add as a codicil the phrase, "and so are the creative." The charm and the irritation inherent in such sweeping generalizations is that while we are not compelled to agree with them, they are surprisingly difficult to disprove. The terms used lead to their own conclusions as is the nature of tautology. For a fleeting moment, however, they ring with the authentic sound of truth.

The linking of wealth and creativity is not pure chance. Artists, for all their anomalous position in our society, can, on occasion, achieve the status of a culture heroine or of a culture hero, as witness Picasso. There is a mystique about the creative individual which is pervasive in our culture today. It is consonant with a profound yearning in Western humankind for transcendental experi-

Alexander Jasnow is a psychotherapist in private practice in Fair Lawn, NJ. For many years he has been interested in the creative process in psychotherapy and in the arts, publishing several papers touching on this area. Mailing address: 14-11 Lucena Dr., Fair Lawn, NJ 07410.

ence at a time when religious faith has been deeply eroded. Art supplies at least the illusion of such transcendence. It is no accident that the self-fulfillment movement of the 1950s and 1960s held out as a major goal the freeing of one's creative potential. If we could not be wealthy or thin, we could at least aspire to being creative.

The desire to identify with the arts and with the artist is of course not new. In the more distant past, we can refer to that frustrated musician, Nero, feverishly seeking the laurel wreath. More recently we can turn to Moliere and his play *"Le Bourgeois Gentilhomme."* His protagonist is a nouveau riche, who aspires to acceptance by polite society. In the pursuit of this goal he engages a tutor to instruct him in the arts, graces, and manners which will gain him the longed-for entry. Picture his joy when he is informed early in his tutelage that he has already mastered an essential art — he can speak prose.

We sophisticates in the audience laugh at this display of ignorance and credulity. We know the difference between everyday prose and poetry even as we assume we know the difference between the prosaic and the creative individual. By simple extrapolation, we assume as psychotherapists that we know the clear distinction between creative and noncreative patients.

However, the attribute of creativity, as is true of so many other human traits, does not lend itself readily to analysis and definition. On the contrary, the deeper we probe, the more complex and elusive it becomes. Is it a unitary trait or composed, as seems more likely, of a number of elements? Is it restricted in its distribution or is it a function of being human? What part does nature play and what is the impact of nurture? To what extent are these traits inherent in the individual and to what extent are they culturally determined and culturally defined? These are basic theoretical issues but obviously these are also questions which have direct relevance to the individual with whom we work.

When we speak of someone as being creative, we imply that this trait, like the trait of intelligence, is potential within the individual. But it is a truism which we encounter in our basic psychology courses, that neither intelligence nor creativity can be measured directly as we measure height and weight. We are compelled to resort to indirect measures using samples of behavior to infer the underlying trait potential. We are left with the nagging questions of the extent to which such samples, and even our choice of samples, are culturally determined. Attempts have been made to develop culture-free tests of intelligence. It is difficult to conceive of a culture-free test of creativity.

To a far greater extent than with intelligence, the perception of what constitutes creative behavior would appear to be culturally and socially determined. If the social determinants in the creative process are as central as I surmise they may be, then this assumption has relevance to our understanding of the creative process in general and of the creative individual in particular.

It is apparent that there is a considerable overlap between the traits of intelligence and creativity. We must consider in fact whether, in separating them as we do, we are not setting up arbitrary and artificial categories. It would certainly seem to be the case that intellectual processes play a central role in creative achievement. We can build a strong argument for the proposition that the highly creative individual is also highly intelligent. The converse proposition, interestingly enough, does not appear to apply. High intelligence does not necessarily appear to carry with it a demonstrably high potential for creative achievement. An interesting question arises: what are the missing ingredients that account for this phenomenon?

In contrast to intelligent behavior which can occur in either a social context or in isolation, it is possible to advance the concept that creative behavior, to a very considerable extent, takes place within a social context. That is to say, while the creative process itself is internalized within the individual and often necessarily takes place in isolation, the process viewed as a whole has essential social precedents and antecedents. Creativity can be perceived as an act of communication. The creative individual may be and often is isolated but connection and communication are implicit and intended in the creative act. The culture supplies the necessary content for the creative artifact or the creative act. For the process to be complete, however, there needs to be a connection with others. In the creative process, there is always an awareness of the other with whom connection is to be made. Even if the existing reality for the creative individual is such that this connection cannot be achieved in the immediate present, the need for and the anticipation of such an ultimate connection continues to be an implicit driving force within the creative process. These considerations as to the social aspect of the creative process have relevance to an approach to the creative patient as well.

In undertaking this project, I decided to select a group of patients whom I considered to be "creative." These I proposed to compare to other patients whom I would not put in this category. I hesitate to use the term "noncreative" in describing the second group because I feel that this term would be misleading. I conceptualize that creativity, like intelligence, is distributed along a continuum. I cannot therefore speak in terms of the presence or absence of creativity any more than I can speak of the presence or absence of intelligence in the individual. Differences between individuals are thought of as differences of degree rather than as differences of kind. Within this context the term noncreative would be a misnomer.

My selective criteria for establishing the groups were pragmatic since the term "creative" had to be very loosely defined. I cast my net rather widely, including those individuals who because of their interests and activities and because of their demonstrated qualities of imagination and originality would generally, in the popular sense of the term, be considered creative.

As stated earlier, I had assumed that even such a casual procedure would still result in two groups with distinct self-evident differences, differences that would be manifest even on cursory examination. That, however, is not quite what transpired.

If anything, from a clinical point of view I was more impressed by the similarities between the groups than by the differences. They appeared to include a similar range of diagnostic categories and a similar range of degree of emotional disturbance. It occurred to me as an afterthought, that I should not have expected otherwise. There is ample documentation from the lives of great artists, that creative individuals are no less prone to emotional disturbance than is the rest of humankind. If anything, the contrary point has often been advanced, that the artist is even more prone to such difficulties than is the majority of humankind. But that is another story.

This preliminary impression of similarity between the two groups still left open the question of what differences, if any, existed between them. To say that one group was demonstrably more creative than the other would be simply going around in a circle since this behavior was itself the selective criterion for group placement. I had the option, as a next step, of approaching the problem more rigorously, more systematically and in greater depth. This would be the logical direction to take. It occurred to me, however, that I still had one further option to explore, even at this preliminary stage. I could raise for myself the question of my own experience in responding to these patients — in short, my own reaction to the individuals in these two groups.

That question was not difficult to answer. The conclusion that surfaced in my mind was that the creative patients were more fun to work with.

I make this statement with, admittedly, a degree of embarrassment. "Fun" is a word that to the best of my knowledge does not have an acceptable place in the professional lexicon. I do not know if Freud ever used it. I am also aware that in presenting my experience in this way, I am revealing as much, if not more, about myself as I am about the patients I work with. This, however, is a risk I must be prepared to undertake.

In the course of therapy we learn, as therapists and as patients (and as therapists, we are always, first, patients), that the road to the understanding and accepting of others is markedly convoluted and involuted. It runs through our understanding and our acceptance of ourselves.

"Fun" is not in the professional lexicon, I assume, because professionals are serious and adult. Fun is for children or for adults playing like children. We can use the term in a pejorative sense accusing the adult of a "childlike" behavior pattern and of not taking a properly serious and responsible attitude toward life and work. Or on the other hand, we can perceive creative individuals, be they emotionally disturbed or not, as having retained a degree of their childhood capacity for play.

I think it is the retained playful potential to which I find myself responding with some feeling of pleasure. Whatever the specific relationship problems being manifested by the patient, whatever the area and degree of conflict and disturbance, we can still make positive contact and we can connect through our mutual interest and pleasure in the play of imagination and in the play of words and ideas.

Perhaps that is one reason why, in my experience, humor so often comes in as an element in the interaction with the creative patient. Humor has its distinctly creative aspect. As in creativity, in humor there is a pleasure to be experienced and shared in the rapid, unexpected, shifting of images and in the unique and original juxtaposition of ideas. The introduction of humor can be seen as an unwarranted and inappropriate intrusion of childlike behavior into a serious enterprise. Or, on the contrary, it can be perceived as a step in the direction of healing, a flexible and sensitive response to the needs and potential of the patient.

The patient's need is for acceptance and affirmation of his meaning as an individual. The creative potential, the capacity for adult play, offers us a further connection point toward the achievement of this goal. Our own capacity, as therapists, to respond to this component in patients' functioning is experienced by them as an affirmation of meaning by the important other. This need for affirmation or confirmation of meaning by others is a crucial aspect of the therapy process in general, but it also plays a specific role in the creative process and therefore in the life of the creative individual.

We can think of the creative process as a process of communication. It is, however, communication of a special kind. We all use language to communicate, language that supplies us with the stock of words and the syntax which is in the public domain. We express our thoughts and needs in the conventional, correct, commonly understood way. We are easily understood by the listener, by the other, to the extent that he or she too has access to the same basic stock of symbols and forms. We are in effect, then, speaking prose.

In the creative process, the individual still utilizes as primary material the content of language, forms, symbols and images which the environment and culture supply. However, in the course of the creative process these are transformed through the creative play into the unique and singular artifacts and behaviors which bear the stamp of originality, which are, in effect, "one of a kind." That is so even though on deeper examination they are invariably seen to have connection with the past since they always draw from the common culture stock which is in the public domain. But originality and uniqueness are never enough. For the creative act to achieve closure there has to be a completion of the act of communication. There is an essential need that others affirm that the created artifact or behavior pattern has meaning. In the absence of such affirmation from others, the creative-act outcome is, in effect, stillborn — the sound of one hand clapping. The creative act is a social act.

It is a social act in spite of the fact that the creative process is an internalized one that takes place in isolation. The solitary writer or painter is nevertheless writing and painting with readers and viewers in mind. The isolation is real but so is the necessity for the "as if" — the potential others who will respond to the work in progress once it is completed, thereby affirming that the communication indeed has meaning. Thus closure of the creative process and of the communication process are simultaneously achieved.

What is pertinent to the creative individual in general is pertinent to the creative patient. This potential for creative play needs to be recognized as a resource because it offers a further contact point in the therapeutic process. The social aspect implicit in the creative process is a driving force within the individual pressing toward connection. Certainly the drive toward connection is an expression of a basic human need. However, in the creative individual the specific form it takes affords an additional leverage point for the therapist.

The puzzling question of why some individuals retain their childhood capacity to play, to imagine, to fantasize, while others do not, at least not to the same degree, still remains to be answered. What about the individuals, however, who retain this capacity but, because of their life experience, feel shy and inhibited about expressing their potential overtly. They may need to experience in their relationship with the therapist that it is acceptable and life-affirming to be playful — that is, creative. I am thinking of the many people who think there is something wrong with them because their thoughts and their perceptions, even their sense of humor, do not conform to the generality. What might be perceived as creative originality in one context might be perceived as bizarre and nonsensical by others. I am reminded of a story by H. G. Wells, I think, of a one-eyed man in a country of the blind. His vision, limited as it was, proved such a handicap to him since it brought him into conflict with others, that he was finally persuaded to give up his remaining vision in order to adapt to his life situation. Such people need the support of the therapist to enable them to reevaluate their self-perception and to become aware that their creative potential is a resource rather than a cause for lowered self-esteem and a barrier to acceptance by others because they are "different."

I have found it useful in working with such individuals to encourage them to bring their creative work into the therapy session. In doing so, I am careful to avoid placing myself in the position of doing a critique of the work. I will state this quite explicitly to avoid the confusion that would ensue if I, as therapist, also undertook the role of the critic. The two roles are in some respect antithetical. I do, however, undertake to explore the work with the patient in the same way that we would explore together a dream or a fantasy that was presented during the therapy hour.

I have found this approach to be generally acceptable and relatively nonthreatening to the patient. It is consistent with the search for meaning which is the constant thrust of the therapy process.

Consider the process of dream work during the therapy hour. So often the dream is offered with an initial defensive statement that it is absurd, it doesn't make sense. How satisfying it is for both the patient and the therapist at the point when they both agree that yes, after all, it does make a great deal of sense.

After all, the goal of achieving meaning pervades the therapeutic enterprise and the creative enterprise as well.

Patients enter therapy as if about to embark on a journey in a search for the meaning which underlies their symptoms, their conflicts, their life as a whole. As therapists we seek to understand our patients. We too are searching for meanings. We may never arrive at the core of meaning but for the therapist as for the patient there is both faith and solace in the assumption that such meaning does exist and is to be found beneath the confusion and uncertainty of each unique life.

Artists, in striving for uniqueness and originality, must transcend the past. In doing so they risk outrunning the possibility of communication and reconnection. They must walk a narrow line. They must be different and yet not so different as to become incomprehensible to others.

Whether for the speaker of prose or of poetry, communication and connection remain basic. The poet may play with words, in effect create a new language, a new syntax. Nevertheless, the meaning of what the poet has to say must be comprehended and affirmed by others or else he or she risks the fate of being left to cry alone in the wilderness.

Our need as therapists is to contact and comprehend our patients whether they speak poetry or prose. The play of the creative patient is serious play. To comprehend this play is both a challenge and a source of pleasure at the creative potential immanent in all human beings.

Creativity and Loneliness

Edward Tick

SUMMARY. Loneliness accompanies creativity. It is necessary in that the creative person must differentiate him/herself from the conforming majority, discover unique purpose, and gather the strength of sensibilities needed to create. But the struggle with loneliness often leads to bitterness, stubbornness, pain, and despair. Further, primitive separation and abandonment issues graft onto present struggles and intermingle with both creativity and personality. The therapeutic challenge is to help the creative client differentiate between loneliness and solitude, treat the loneliness while strengthening the solitude, differentiate and treat accordingly ordinary disorders and the unusual psychic phenomena necessary to creativity.

Innumerable passages in the literature of creativity testify to the creative person's struggle with loneliness. This is as it must be, for the creative person is inherently at odds with the mass of individuals who seek life-styles of conformity and adjustment, participating in creativity secondarily as audience or unconsciously through their dreams. But for the creative person, the inwardly felt pressure to express oneself is paramount, even at the cost of struggle, isolation, loneliness, agony, despair.

In our form of culture, one's contribution to the marketplace determines one's worth to the community. In such a climate, the creative person, whose work cannot be measured by marketability, is likely to feel worthless, detached, unsupported by the general community. One is likely to develop the sense of being an "outsider," much written about in existential literature. This outsider status comes with the territory of creativity; the creative person must struggle with loneliness as an *a priori* condition of creativity. As therapists, we must seek at once, to affirm the necessity of solitude

Edward Tick, PhD, holds degrees in psychology, communication, and literature. He is in private practice in Columbia County and Albany, NY, and in addition, is a poet and writer. Mailing address: 714 Myrtle Ave., Albany, NY 12208.

to the creator and at the same time to differentiate it from loneliness, struggling with and against the loneliness to turn it from enemy into friend.

Albert Camus was one of four century's foremost spokespeople for the dignity of the solitary human being confronting our dehumanizing times. He confided his struggle with loneliness to his journals. In his notes on the composition of *The Plague* (Camus, 1970) he wrote, "Each man seeks his desert, and as soon as he is there finds it too harsh. It shall not be said that I cannot bear my own" (p. 226). Here Camus reflects that in order to find ourselves, we must each withdraw to a desert, a wilderness, and confront our individual natures. This necessary withdrawal is expressed throughout the literary and sacred books of the world. Jesus' sojourn in the wilderness; the Buddha's forsaking his throne and, later, his meditation under the Bo Tree; Odysseus' solitary 10-year voyage of trials on the way to his homeland; Nietzsche's solitude and his character Zarathustra's withdrawal to the mountain; Ishmael's lone survival in *Moby Dick* are all prime examples.

Such withdrawal is an utter necessity in the evolution of the creator. Its primacy is alluded to in the notion of God the Creator alone in an undifferentiated universe before the Genesis. Camus notes, "Myself, that is to say this intense emotion which frees me from my surroundings" (p. 237). It is only by separating that one can discover one's true nature and purpose and gather the full intensity of one's emotions and sensibilities that are needed to create. But the problem is, as Camus says, that once in that wilderness, most people find it unbearable and free from it—often, today, into the therapist's office. Only the creators, the saints, the insane remain.

Another Nobel Prize-winning writer, the Greek poet George Seferis (1975), likewise confided his struggles with loneliness to his journals. His thoughts confirm Camus' regarding the pain of the struggle to be alone with heightened and therefore abnormal sensibilities:

> I think that lately . . . I have suffered the worst that could have happened to me in the times we live in: a flood of sensitivity makes me feel as if, stripped of protective skin, I'm wandering about with open wounds. Dust, flies, awkward gestures — all very painful . . . I long for the days I could sometimes control this sensitivity with grace . . . Yet I feel this condition is not sickness, it's an ardent affirmation of life. There's no lack of

courage, the calm surface hasn't changed, but a terrible effort
is needed, which makes me lamentably heavyhearted. (pp. 83-
84)

The person driven to create must withdraw from conformity.
Only in such withdrawal will one's thoughts, emotions, and sensibilities be heightened to the pitch necessary to allow the world to
flow through the self in artistic expression. But that very withdrawal, however necessary, is a terrible burden to bear, one from
which most people flee and which often affects the creative person
by making him or her stubborn, somber, "lamentably heavyhearted," weary, depressed, hypersensitive, hyperalert. Camus
(1970) wrote, "Let the man who is alone at least keep his scorn,
and the ability to pick out from this terrible ordeal what serves his
own greatness" (p. 252). The creative person may be full of scorn
and bitterness, feel inadequately understood and appreciated; and is
likely to rely on his or her own critical judgments, believing that,
again in Camus' words, "The first thing to do is to keep silent —
abolish audiences and learn to be your own judge" (p. 245).

These conditions, inherent in the struggle to create, pose unique
problems for the psychotherapist. Weariness, scorn, bitterness, hy-
persensitivity may be judged by the therapist to be symptoms in
need of treatment rather than accompaniments to a state deserving
preservation and strengthening. This conflict was portrayed in Peter
Shaffer's (1974) play *Equus* in which a psychiatrist, curing a young
man of the passions and hallucinations that marked his madness,
also initiated the loss of his patient's creativity and sensitivity. It is
an age-old problem for therapists — how to treat the remarkably sensitive without harming their remarkability. And creative people are
aware of the conflict, approaching therapists with fear and trembling lest they lose the very traits by which they define themselves.
The poet Rainer Maria Rilke once considered psychoanalysis. The
analyst he consulted explained that therapy would only lead to the
disappearance of Rilke's devils. Rilke declined treatment, stating
that if he lost his devils he was afraid he would lose his angels as
well.

All the struggles of the lonely patient will be present in the creative patient, intensified by the creative process itself, by the necessary withdrawal which cannot be ameliorated by ordinary strate-

gies, and by the self-justifying tendencies of the creative person that say, in effect, that "therapeutic standards apply to others but not to me because I am special."

The problems of loneliness have been summarized in these pages by E. Mark Stern (1986) and can be valuably applied to the problems of treating creative patients:

> In the lonely person, objects, places, and persons exist only as fading echoes of an equally fading self. As an expression of boundary loss, loneliness heightens the experience of not knowing where one is. It is as if one's frustration equals abandonment, while the other person's negligence corresponds to contemptuousness. (p. 1)

In the creative as well as in the lonely person, ego boundaries are fading away. In order for the world to emerge through the self, they must fade. It is often only the saving grace of the creative work itself that defines ego boundaries for the creative individual. And in the transition period from withdrawal to active creative work, the creator may truly not know where she or he is and will not be fully in the shared world. Rather, the creator will be existing, simultaneously and with greater than normal intensity and frustration, in the shared world and the inner dreamlike world of the imagination.

Frustration coupled with boundary loss will often be experienced as abandonment. That abandonment will be sublimated onto present-day issues and themes: why can't I get published? sell my paintings? get good reviews? In fact, while these may be true problems, they gather all the energy of the creator's original separation and abandonment experiences to them. Then, "negligence corresponds to contemptuousness" and the creative person fills with bitterness and scorn. She or he is unaware that the world is unaware of him or her as a struggling human being. Instead, ignorance is interpreted as contempt, abandonment, betrayal, with all the pain and rage and fear of an infant unanswered in the crib.

Stern continues:

> What is often seen as unavailable is often unreal. What results is a secret envy or foiled longing prompting a mode of poverty that bonds individuals to a sense of despair. . . . Idealized projections, representatives of another's claim to popularity,

remain in the forefront. Loneliness, by necessity, feeds on such models. [Such] individuals . . . safeguard their illusions of thwarted entitlement. (p. 1)

The creative person, burning with inner fires and believing that the stories, sights, or sounds one creates can, indeed, change the world if only others would see or hear, is in an impossible position. Seeing or hearing other worlds, one cannot see that fame and fortune are unreal, unavailable, "idealized projections." Many creative clients will feel falsely and grandly entitled. This will be so in part because of frustration with the time lag between creating a work and its reception in the community, in part because this "thwarted entitlement," "secret envy," "foiled longing" emerges out of loneliness itself and carries with it all the primitive associations and emotions of early thwarted longings. Here it is well to remember Freud's concept of a neurosis of destiny in which, Freud stated, one convinced of a higher and promised destiny is compensating for hidden early feelings of extreme negligence and deprivation. The therapist must affirm the real aspects of foiled longing and unavailable fame. The therapist must also help the creative client uncover the real early feelings and memory traces leading to the pressure to achieve with one's creations that, it is wished, will finally get all the world to love the creator. Such impossible longings do, indeed, "bond individuals to a sense of despair." There are endless affirmations by creative people of the degree of foiled longing and despair with which they coexist. Here, then, despair must be treated not as a permanent condition of existence but rather as a feeling state that can be altered. As Camus wrote in a "Letter to a man in despair,"

I cease to agree with you when you try to base your life on this despair, maintain that everything is equally pointless, and withdraw behind your disgust. For despair in a feeling, and not a permanent condition. You cannot live on despair. And this feeling must give way to a clear view of things. (p. 253)

Indeed, on the other side of despair, if the creative person can pass through its hellfires, is "a clear view of things," a view sometimes obtained by spiritual pilgrims but only rarely by creative persons. In fact, it is only when despair is overcome and the creative person's self becomes "full of world," to paraphrase the poet Cesar Vallejo, that creativity is enlisted in the service of humanity rather than of the ego. So the battle against despair, often carried out in the psychotherapeutic journey, is, with the creative patient, a battle to wrest creativity from the limited service of the ego in order to dedicate it to the service of the world at large. Camus again: "And when am I truer and more transparent than when I *am* the world?" (p. 238).

In the opening pages of his autobiography, Thomas Merton (1952), a religious seeker who was also a poet and who was the child of artist-parents, lamented, "The integrity of the artist lifts a man above the level of the world without delivering him from it" (p. 11). This expresses the root conflict in struggling with the loneliness of creative clients. Forsaking the usual comforts, securities, and attachments that confirm, bound, and solidity our existences in the common world we share with others, the creative client must come, like the spiritual seeker, to attach himself or herself to higher visions and purposes, the radiant presence of the sensual world as it can be gained through creativity.

The therapist must help the creative person preserve both angels and devils in such a manner that they do not torture or block creativity. The therapist must also help the creative person differentiate between loneliness and solitude. This differentiation corresponds to "the two faces of selflessness," wherein the first is emptiness, developmental deficit, lack of connection; and the second is a mature and conscious donation of self to higher purpose (Stern, 1985/6; Travers, 1985/6). It is, indeed, creative solitude that is the necessary condition. Loneliness is, as it were, the social disease. Lord Byron sang, "In solitude, when I am least alone . . .", and Yeats exhorted, "Be secret and exalt . . ." The twin struggles of the creative person are, therefore, to embrace both angels and devils without becoming mad; and to embrace solitude and manage loneliness so that they do not distort, embitter, or block one's creativity or personality.

The challenges to the therapist are to guide the client in solitude while carefully treating the loneliness; to differentiate between ordinary disorders and those psychic phenomena necessary for the creative act to come to pass; to manage therapeutic encounters with such sensitivity that creativity is affirmed while disorderedness is treated. This is a most demanding task, one that resists ordinary theories and approaches. But it is a creative act, and in it the therapist can become a rare and special kind of creative friend, expressed by poet Louis Hammer (1985, p. 50) in this way:

Here is the friend
who comes where the light
works around the earth

the friend comes
to cure us of being

he stands in our light

the friend is the game
of slipping between light and time

We may stand in that light long enough to help our creative clients live in time, but never long enough to rob them of their gift of sight.

REFERENCES

Camus, A. (1970). *Selected essays and notebooks*. Middlesex, England: Penguin.

Hammer, L. (1985). *The book of games*. Old Chatham, NY: Sachem Press.

Merton, T. (1952). *The seven storey mountain*. New York: Signet.

Seferis, G. (1975). *A poet's journal: Days of 1945-1951*. Cambridge, MA: Harvard University Press.

Shaffer, P. (1974). *Equus*. New York: Avon Books.

Stern, E.M. (1985/6). Selflessness as enlargement of being. *The Psychotherapy Patient, 2*(2), xi-xiii.

Stern, E.M. (1986). Loneliness and the fuller vision. *The Psychotherapy Patient, 2*(3), 1-2.

Travers, J.A. (1985/6). Two faces of selflessness. *The Psychotherapy Patient, 2*(2), 3-10.

Hemispheric Specialization
and Creativity in Psychotherapy

Klaus D. Hoppe
Neville L. Kyle

SUMMARY. The neuropsychological basis of interhemispheric (or transcallosal) communication and hemispheric specialization is discussed in terms of creativity. An experimental application utilizing a standardized questionnaire with patients in the course of their psychotherapy is presented with results related to a normal control group and to more or less creative patients. Therapeutic applications such as information giving, biofeedback, dreams, fantasies, and resymbolization are noted along with potential applications in psychotherapy and education.

COMMISSUROTOMY AND TRANSCALLOSAL
COMMUNICATION

Since the epochal work on split-brain patients of the Nobel Laureate Roger Sperry and his associates (Sperry, Gazzaniga, & Bo-

Klaus D. Hoppe, MD, PhD, graduated and received his postdoctoral training as psychiatrist and psychoanalyst in Berlin, Germany. Since 1960, he has been Director of Research and Continuing Medical Education at the Hacker Clinic, Los Angeles and Lynwood, CA; since 1971, he has been Associate Professor of Clinical Psychiatry at UCLA. Dr. Hoppe's 60 publications consist in numerous papers and chapters on experimental headache, on survivors of the Holocaust, on split-brain and alexithymia, as well as a book in German on Psychiatry and Religion. Mailing address: 6399 Wilshire Blvd. #414, Los Angeles, CA 90048.

Neville L. Kyle, PhD, graduated with doctoral degree from the University of Nottingham, England in 1964. For the past 16 years he has been Chief of Psychological Services at the Hacker Clinic in Lynwood, CA. Dr. Kyle has written, spoken, and published in various areas including experimental therapy with skin disorder, survivors of severe persecution, test characteristics of skyjackers, post-traumatic stress disorder, and biofeedback training. Mailing address: 3621 E. Century Blvd., #11, Lynwood, CA 90262.

The authors gratefully acknowledge the assistance of Warren TenHouten, PhD, of the Department of Sociology at UCLA, in the section on Data Analysis.

139

gen, 1969; Benson & Zaidel, 1985; Bogen, 1985) recognition of the different functions of the left and right cerebral hemispheres has become essential to the understanding of our mental capacities.

The left hemisphere is specialized for the comprehension and production of speech and writing, as well as for a mode of information processing that has been variously described as linear, analytic, systematic, sequential, objective, nonrepresentational, or externally focused.

The right hemisphere, on the other hand, while playing a role in speech intonation and gestures, is specialized for timbre, facial recognition, and the perception and manipulation of spatial relations. More generally, the right hemisphere is specialized for a mode of information processing variously described as nonlinear, synthetic, structural, simultaneous, subjective, representational, or internally focused. The right hemisphere senses the forest, so to speak, while the left hemisphere often cannot see the woods for the trees.

Our earlier clinical observations on 12 "commissurotomy" or "split-brain" patients (Hoppe, 1977, 1978; Hoppe & Bogen, 1977) have been experimentally confirmed: in comparison to eight matched control subjects, patients with cerebral commissurotomy used significantly fewer affect-laden words and adjectives, used a higher percentage of auxiliary words, and produced significantly more incomplete sentences. Commissurotomy patients tended not to fantasize about, imagine, or interpret symbols; and they also tended to describe the circumstances surrounding events, as opposed to describing their own feelings about these events. On a global level, commissurotomy patients tended to symbolize in a discursive, logically articulated style, using mainly a secondary process; they showed a concreteness of symbolization, and the quality of their symbolizations emphasized stereotyped denotations. Apparently the loss of transcallosal communications between the two hemispheres caused a lack of affect-laden verbalization, of fantasies and symbolization, as well as the occurrence of alexithymia (TenHouten, Hoppe, Bogen, & Walter, 1985, 1986).

Joseph Bogen, Sperry's closest coworker and neurosurgeon of the "split-brain" patients, together with his wife Glenda, emphasized a role for the corpus callosum in creativity (Bogen & Bogen, 1969). The functioning of the corpus callosum is "associated with the highest and most elaborate activities of the brain." If transcallosal interhemispheric exchange is blocked, the result is a lack of creativity. Bogen (1969) attributes a lack of creativity to various factors, including a transcallosal inhibition of the right hemisphere by the dominant left hemisphere. This may explain how failure to develop fresh insights in the outside world is closely related to a lack of further insight into one's "other" self. The artist needs an openness toward the "other side of the brain."

Bogen and Bogen (1977) amplified their original ideas (Bogen & Bogen, 1969) by postulating a two-phase process of creativity with regard to the cerebral hemispheres. In the first phase, there is a relative paucity of interhemispheric communication; both hemispheres can thus independently develop their own processes without too much interference. The second phase consists of a temporary establishment of a more free access and communication between the two hemispheres. At that particular time, imagery or configuration, generated in the right hemisphere, can be realized through the left hemisphere.

In our experimental study of eight split-brain patients and eight normal control subjects, TenHouten, Hoppe, Bogen, & Walter, 1985) we used as stimulus a film consisting of affect-laden symbols. The different reaction of alexithymic split-brain patients and expressive-creative control subjects corresponds with the different form of symbolization in both hemispheres.

According to Susan Langer (1942) discursive symbolization is articulated and needs a secondary thought process (Reality Principle, Freud, 1911/1958). Presentational symbolization represents a logic of feelings, as expressed in fine art, mystical experiences, or music; and exhibits primary process attributes, such as condensation and displacement.

In expressive-creative people, the presentational symbolization and imagery in the right hemisphere is available to the left hemisphere via the corpus callosum. The transformational process of verbalizing presentational symbols was called "symbollexia" by Klaus D. Hoppe (1985, 1986). Commissurotomy/split-brain patients lack symbollexia. Their predominantly discursive symbolization in the left hemisphere corresponds with alexithymia in people who haven't been operated on but function in a similar way ("functional commissurotomy," Hoppe, 1977, 1978, 1984).

Creativity depends on the transformational intercallosal process of symbollexia. The question remains: What facilitates that creative moment? What combines primary and secondary process to the "magic synthesis" of a tertiary process (Arieti, 1976)?

By using Koestler's (1964) ingenious concept of bisociation, we could call creativity a *hemispheric bisociation*. Whereas the left hemisphere follows the fixed set of rules, this code governs the matrix of an overwhelming possibility of choices expressed by the right hemisphere. The "magic synthesis" of the two cerebral planes is the creative process of hemispheric bisociation. As Koestler (1978) put it: "By living on both planes at once, the creative artist or scientist is able to catch an occasional glimpse of eternity looking through the window of time" (p. 146).

One therapeutic goal consists of combining the view through the window of outside time (*erlebte Zeit*, Hoppe, 1978; or clock time, Loye, 1983), registered in the left hemisphere, with the view through the window of inner time experiences (*gelebte Zeit*, Hoppe, 1978; or spatial time, Loye, 1983), mainly experienced in the right hemisphere.

With regard to feelings, it should be stressed that emotions, which are generated in the two closely linked limbic systems, are not simply lateralized on the right side. The cognitive representations of emotions (feelings and symbols) are also represented in both hemispheres. However, there exists experimental evidence suggesting that the right hemisphere plays a special role in perceptual judgment of a variety of affect-laden stimuli (Carmon & Nachson, 1973; Haggard & Parkinson, 1971; Safer & Leventhal, 1977; Tucker et al., 1976; Wechsler, 1973). Ley and Bryden (1981) have found that emotional stimuli are perceived more accurately when presented to the right hemisphere, which suggests that the right hemisphere has a special and prominent influence on the reception and expression of emotions.

From a clinical point of view, alexithymia (Sifneos, 1973) or "functional commissurotomy" (Hoppe, 1977, 1978, 1984) is the opposite of creativity. In the following, applications of this understanding in psychotherapy will be demonstrated by the use of the Hemispheric Consensus Prediction Profile Test (Loye, 1984).

EXPERIMENTAL APPLICATIONS

Instrument: Hemispheric Consensus Prediction Profile Test (HCP)

Purpose

The HCP Profile test was developed by Loye at UCLA (1983) and based on item analyses of a 40-item test run on several sample groups to determine those subjects who are hypothetical right or left brain dominant. It also purports to identify those subjects who, to some appreciable degree, draw upon *both* hemispheres in problem solving.

Method

The control group for this study was 18 Catholic priests attending a workshop on Spiritual-Emotional Integration. Their scores on the HCP Profile test were compared with 35 patients in various stages of psychotherapy, 19 of whom were Catholic priests. The educational level and ages were approximately the same for both patient and control group.

Results

1. The priest control group tended to be higher in left-hemisphere dominance than did the patient group. The mean left-hemisphere score for controls as 12.66, for patient groups it was 10.81.
2. The priest controls used both hemispheric functions more than did the patients: i.e., mean score = 7.17 compared to 5.37.
3. In a second step of this study, the 35 patients were divided by their therapist (senior author KDH) into relatively *creative* patients and *alexithymic* (relatively noncreative) patients. This procedure resulted in a group of 19 relatively *creative* patients and 16 relatively *alexithymic* patients for which HCP Profile test results were compared.

   a. *Creative* patients were found to be more right-hemisphere oriented than *alexithymic* patients: i.e., mean score = 12.11 compared to 4.18.
   b. The *creative* priest-patients used *both* hemispheric functions to a greater degree than did the alexithymic priest-patients: i.e., mean score = 6.12 compared to 5.13.
   c. To explore these obtained relationships further, a group of seven patients identified by their therapist as *extremely* alexithymic, and a group of four patients identified as *extremely* creative were compared. The extremely creative patients did differ a great deal in terms of more right-than left-brain usage (mean score = 15.5 to 3.42). While creative patients in general used *both* hemispheres more than alexithymic patients, the obtained difference was not large (7.5 to 6.42).

Data Analysis

The first stage of data analysis consisted of a study of the 20 HCP questionnaire items intended to measure right/left-hemisphere preference among subjects in two experimental groups and one control group. Four of the items were not consistently correlated with the others and were discarded. The remaining items were subjected to alpha common factor analysis. Here two pairs of variables were negatively correlated; these four items also had negative pattern matrix coefficients and were also deleted.

In the next 12 variable analysis two additional items had negative one-factor pattern matrix coefficients and were also discarded. This process of deleting inconsistent items was continued until an eight-variable, one-factor solution was obtained. Results of this analysis are shown in Table 1.

The Heise-Bohrnstedt inter-item reliability coefficient of .81 indicated that the eight retained items can be interpreted as parallel measures for the same latent concept (Heise & Bohrnstedt, 1970).

A measure of right-hemisphere preference was derived by standardizing each of the eight variables, weighing them by their factor score coefficient, and then adding these products. The resulting indicator is termed RIGHT.[1]

In the next step the three groups (control, patient non-priests, and patient priests) were used as three levels of a factor predicting RIGHT in a one-way analysis of variance. The GROUP factor was not a significant predictor of RIGHT.

The contrast between the two patient groups was of particular importance because for the priests and non-priests groups measures

TABLE 1

CORRELATION MATRIX

ITEM	A1	A2	A3	B4	B5	B6	B7	FACTOR MATRIX
A2	.47							3.75
A3	.66	.50						3.13
B4	.35	.26	.37					2.57
B5	.67	.36	.70	.30				1.24
B6	.29	.21	.32	.23	.26			1.22
B7	.43	.35	.54	.41	.40	.18		.67
B8	.66	.43	.62	.29	.54	.49	.54	.55
TOTAL								13.13

had been obtained for alexithymia (high alexithymia = "2", alexithymia = "1", non-alexithymia = "0").

A regression type analysis of covariance was carried out. To assess the significance of the factor-covariate interactions the variance was explained using the two *interactional terms*, the two covariates, and the dichotomous factor compared in a second analysis not including the factor-covariate variables. The change in R^2, in going from five to three variables, (from .48 to .41), was significant: $F(2,47) = 3.68$, $p < .05$. The group-creative term (GC) was significant, $\beta = 1.37$, $t = 2.39$, $p = .02$, but the group alexithymia term (GA) was not.

A second regression analysis included GC, ALEXITHYMIA, CREATIVE, and GROUP. Here the covariate ALEXITHYMIA was significant ($\beta = -.419$, $t = -3.46$, $p = .001$) but CREATIVE was not.

A third analysis used GC, ALEXITHYMIA and GROUP. Here GC and ALEXITHYMIA emerged as significant but GROUP, again, was not. A fourth analysis was done with GC and ALEXITHYMIA. Here both variables remained significant in their effects on RIGHT (for GC, $\beta = .48$, $t = 3.90$, $p = .001$; for ALEXITHYMIA, $\beta = -.38$, $t = -3.18$, $p = .002$).

These results indicate that alexithymic patients were less apt to utilize right-hemisphere modes than were less alexithymic subjects. The significant interaction GC indicated that with these groups the effects of creativity depends on patient group membership (i.e., priest, non-priest). The slope of the regression of RIGHT on CREATIVITY was significantly higher for the priest patients ($\beta = .85$, $t = 6.16$, $p < .0001$), than for the non-priests ($\beta = .72$, $t = 4.28$, $p < .001$). The corresponding adjusted R^2's are priests .71 and non-priests .49. That is, the tendency for creative priests to use the right-hemisphere mode was more pronounced than among the creative non-priest patients.

Conclusions

Among other things, these results indicate that:

1. Alexithymics were significantly less apt to show a right-hemisphere orientation on the HCP than were non-alexithymics;
2. There is a significant tendency for the more creative patients to show a right-hemisphere orientation. This was found in both patient groups, but was significantly stronger among the priests than the non-priests.

Larger sample sizes may well have resulted in more clear-cut differences among other variables of this study, such as in the use of *both* hemisphere items; justification for the use of these sample sizes in a clinical study is given in several texts (see Smith, 1983).

THERAPEUTIC APPLICATIONS

Information

During the course of psychotherapy, according to their particular stage, our patients were asked to fill out the HCP Profile and subsequently informed about the results and the differences of right- and left-brain functions. This information giving was followed by an attempt to work through marked imbalances between the two hemispheric styles and to stimulate more creative processes.

The realization of predominant hemispheric style was not only helpful to the patient but also sometimes to the understanding of the significant other in their life. For example, a very creative female patient persistently complained about the lack of intellectual and emotional communication with her husband. After she had completed her profile, she took another home for her husband to fill out. The dramatic difference between her predominantly right-hemispheric and her husband's predominantly left-hemispheric profile provided a basis for greater understanding and tolerance for the different style of thinking, feeling, and communication.

Relaxation, Autogenic Training, Biofeedback

At our clinic, with those patients who were undergoing combined relaxation, autogenic training, and biofeedback training, an increased tendency to report emotional-related responses has been noted during the course of their treatment. These findings correspond with the pioneering and ongoing research of the Langley Porter Institute in San Francisco. While Ornstein (1972) wrote on the psychology of consciousness and altered states, more recent work includes the use of EEG brainwave and analyses providing both analog and digital tone feedback. Through biofeedback, training subjects are able to produce a state of "synchronization" or "resonance" between the two brain hemispheres. As Loye (1983) put it: "Flashes of creative insight have been reported often by participants who have learned to sustain relatively uninterrupted synchronous bilateral EEG patterns" (p. 275).

Similar effects are reported from several sources from subjects undergoing relaxation and autogenic training in conjunction with biofeedback (Woolfolk & Lehrer, 1984).

Fantasies, Dreams and Free Associations

It could be observed that patients who had difficulties in associating and in recollecting dreams and fantasies were predominantly using left-hemispheric thinking according to their HCP profile. After a discussion of the HCP results, these patients were more aware of their intellectual-emotional blocks and motivated to be more open to free associations, dreams, and fantasies represented in their right hemisphere.

Resymbolization

Especially in the priest-patient group, the process of resymbolization was stressed (Hoppe, 1984). The transformation of presentational symbols from the right hemisphere via symbollexia to the left hemisphere enriches not only the private life of the particular priest but also his liturgy and prayer life ("inner speech," Hoppe, 1985).

As mentioned in the introduction, presentational symbolization and imagery is closely linked with feelings. In contrast, exclusive discursive symbolization is prone to become arid, concrete, and rigid. Symbols are changed into signs which lose their emotional meaning and replace warm communications, vitality, and spontaneity.

For example, one priest whose psychotherapy was described in detail (Hoppe, 1984) was able to balance his right- and left-hemispheric thinking. By gaining insight and openness toward symbols and feelings, this patient was able to develop a vital balance between the cortical styles of his left and right hemisphere. He enjoyed his leisure time, the beauty of nature, and was living more according to his "inner time" experience. He developed communication with copriests and parishioners and introduced symbolic elements into the church liturgy.

Guided Imagery

"Initial symbol projection" or "guided imagery" (Leuner, 1966, 1970) is another important parameter in the psychotherapy of those patients who are predominantly using left-hemispheric thinking. In the last phase of his many-years-long psychoanalytically-oriented psychotherapy, a very intelligent patient who predominantly used his left hemisphere was asked to imagine himself to be on a meadow and from there to enter a forest where he was digging up a treasure box under a tree. He associated as his finding a necklace and spontaneously decided to make it a gift to his wife. When this was carried out in a real life situation, it improved their relationship and marriage.

CONCLUSIONS

The theoretical and practical applications of the new knowledge about hemispheric specialization opens a new dimension in psychotherapy, especially concerning the issue of creativity. Based on our clinical experiences and experimental findings with the HCP Profile, it can be stated that transcallosal "symbollexia" and "hemispheric bisociation" may be most useful concepts in a broad variety of psychotherapeutic applications.

In our present study, the tendency to use both hemispheres together, in HCP Profile terms, was somewhat more characteristic of the normal control group, while bilateral usage of hemispheres also characterized the more creative patients. This effect, while not statistically significant, was in contrast to the significantly less right-hemisphere usage on the part of the more alexithymic patients; the more creative patient experimental group tended to use the right hemisphere in preference to the left to a significant degree.

Clinically, in our patient groups the following specific applications have been found useful: giving information about hemispheric specialization, enhanced imagery, and expression of affect through relaxation and autogenic training, fantasies, dreams, free associations, resymbolizations, and guided imagery.

We may envision future research and therapeutic applications in such directions as the perennial problem of blockages (i.e., writers block) experienced by truly creative persons such as writers and artists, as Marilee Zdenek (1983) has recounted so richly in reports of her workshop on the Right Brain Experience.

Another field of important applications for this work is within the public educational system in the United States. Both Bogen (1975) and Sperry (1985) have noted this urgent need in public education. As Sperry put it:

> The amount of formal training given to right hemisphere functions in our public schools traditionally has been almost negligible, compared to that devoted to the specialties of the left hemisphere. The need for better methods by which to detect, measure, and develop the non-verbal components of intellect before their critical development periods have passed in becoming widely recognized. (p. 18)

Our present approach is both based on and is intended to reflect the philosophy of applied neuropsychology evinced by Roger Sperry (1985) who stated:

> The change is away from the mechanistic, deterministic, and reductionistic doctrines of pre-1965 science to the more humanistic interpretation of the 1970s. Our current views are more mentalistic, holistic, and subjectivistic. They give more freedom in that they reduce the restriction of mechanistic determinism, and they are more rich in quality, value, and meaning. (p. 24)

NOTE

1. The eight RIGHT indicator items of the HCP:

A1. Do you tend to get at solutions to problems by: (1) analyzing them step by step. Or by (2) getting a "feel" for the solution all of a sudden, as a whole.
A2. For you is it more fun to: (1) plan realistically, or (2) dream.
A3. Do you respond more to people when: (1) they appeal to your reason, or (2) when they appeal to your emotions.
B4. Do you work best at: (1) improving something. Or by (2) inventing something.
B5. When confronted with a new situation, do you tend to: (1) carefully analyze it before acting. Or (2) rely on first impressions or feelings and go ahead.
B6. When you work on projects, do you most want them to be: (1) well-planned. Or (2) designed to contribute something new.
B7. In regard to your work or personal life, do you generally follow hunches if they are: (1) supported by logic. Or (2) have the right "feel."
B8. In dealing with a problem, which gives you the most satisfaction: (1) solving it by thinking it through. Or (2) tieing fascinating ideas together.

REFERENCES

Arieti, S. (1976). *Creativity, the magic synthesis*. New York: Basic Books.

Benson, D.S., & Zaidel, E. (Eds.). (1985). *The dual brain. Hemispheric specialization in humans*. New York: The Guilford Press.

Bogen, J.E. (1969). The other side of the brain: II. An appositional mind. *Bulletin Los Angeles Neurologic Society, 34*, 135-162.

Bogen, J.E. (1975). Some educational aspects of hemispheric specialization. *UCLA Educator, 17*, 24-32.

Bogen, J.E. (1985). The callosal syndromes. In P.M. Heilman, B. Valenstein (Eds.), *Clinical Neuropsychology* (2nd ed., 295-338). New York, Oxford: Oxford University Press.

Bogen, J.E., & Vogel, P.J. (1962). Cerebral commissurotomy in man: Preliminary case report. *Bulletin Los Angeles Neurologic Society, 27*, 169-172.

Bogen, J.E., & Bogen, G.M. (1969). The other side of the brain: III. The corpus callosum and creativity. *Bulletin Los Angeles Neurologic Society, 31*, 191-220.

Bogen, J.E., & Bogen, G.M., (1977, Oct.). Some further thoughts on the corpus callosum and creativity. Seminar at the Chicago Institute for Psychoanalysis.

Carmon, A., & Nachson, I. (1973). Ear asymmetry in perception of emotional non-verbal stimuli. *Acta Psychologica, 37*, 351-357.

Freud, S. (1958). formulations on the two principles on mental functioning. In J. Strachey (Ed. and Trans.), *The standard edition of the complete psychological works of Sigmund Freud* (Vol. 12, pp. 219-226). London: Hogarth Press. (Original work published 1911).

Haggard, M.P., & Parkinson, A.M. (1971). Stimulus on task factors as determinants of ear advantages. *Quarterly Journal of Experimental Psychology, 23*, 168-177.

Heise, D.R., & Bohrnstedt, G.W. (1970). Validity, invalidity, and reliability. In E.F. Borgatta & G.W. Bohrnstedt (Eds.), *Sociological Methodology* (pp. 104-129). San Francisco: Jossey-Bass.

Hoppe, K.D. (1977). Split brains and psychoanalysis. *Psychoanalytic Quarterly, 46*, 220-244.

Hoppe, K.D. (1978). Split-brain—psychoanalytic findings and hypotheses. *Journal of the American Academy of Psychoanalysis, 6*, 193-213.

Hoppe, K.D. (1984). Severed ties. In *Psychoanalytic reflections on the holocaust: Selected essays* (pp. 94-111). New York: KATV Publishing House.

Hoppe, K.D. (1984). Psychoanalysis and Christian religion: Past views and new findings. *Bulletin of the National Guild of Catholic Psychiatrists, 30*, 20-42.

Hoppe, K.D. (1985). Mind and spirituality: Symbollexia, empathy and God-representation. *Bulletin of the National Guild of Catholic Psychiatrists, 31*, 10-23.

Hoppe, K.D. (1986). Dialogue of the future. In L. Robinson (Ed.), *Psychiatry and religion: Overlapping concerns* (pp. 120-132). Washington, DC: Monograph Series of American Psychiatric Press.

Hoppe, K.D., & Bogen, J.E. (1977). Alexithymia in twelve commissurotomized patients. *Psychotherapy-Psychosomatics, 28*, 148-255.

Koestler, A. (1978). *Janus*. New York: Random House.

Koestler, A. (1964). *The act of creation*, New York: McMillan.

Langer, S. (1942). *Philosophy in a new key*. Cambridge, MA: Harvard University Press.

Leuner, H. (1966). *The use of initiated symbol projection in psychotherapy*. A lecture sponsored by the Sections of Experimental Psychology, New Jersey, Bureau of Research in Neurology and Psychiatry, Princeton, NJ.

Leuner, H. (1970). *Katathymes Bilderleben*. Stuttgart: Thieme.

Ley, R.G., & Bryden, M.P. (1981). Consciousness, emotion, and the right hemisphere. In G. Underwood & R. Stevens, (Eds.), *Aspects of consciousness* (Vol. 2). London: Academic Press.

Loye, D. (1983). *The sphinx and the rainbow*. New Science Library, Boulder & London: Shambala.

Loye, D. (1983). The brain, the mind and the future. *Technological Forecasting and Social Change, 27*, 267-280.

Ornstein, R. (1972). *The psychology of consciousness*. San Francisco: W. H. Freeman & Co.

Safes, M.A., & Leventhal, H. (1977). Ear differences in evaluating emotional tones of voice and verbal content. *Journal of Experimental Psychology, 3*, 75-82.

Sifneos, P. (1973). The prevalence of "alexithymia," characteristics in psychosomatic patients. *Psychotherapy-Psychosomatics, 28*, 255-263.

Smith, K. (1983). Tests of significance: Some frequent misunderstandings, *American Journal of Orthopsychiatry, 53*(2), 315-321.

Sperry, R. (1985). Consciousness, personal identity and the divided brain. In D.F. Benson & E. Zaidel (Eds.), *The dual brain*, (pp. 11-25). New York: Guilford Press.

Sperry, R., Gazzaniga, M., & Bogen, J.E. (1969). Interhemispheric relationship; the neocortical commissures: Syndromes of hemispheric disconnection. In *Handbook of clinical neurology* (Vol. 4, pp. 278-290). Amsterdam: New Holland.

TenHouten, W.D., Hoppe, K.D., Bogen, J.E., & Walter, D.O. (1985). Alexithymia and the split brain I, Lexical-level content analysis. *Psychotherapy-Psychosomatics, 43*, 202-208.

TenHouten, W.D., Hoppe, K.D., Bogen, J.E., & Walter, D.O. (1985). Alexithymia and the split brain II, Sentential-level content analysis. *Psychotherapy-Psychosomatics, 44*, 1-5.

TenHouten, W.D., Hoppe, K.D., Bogen, J.E., & Walter, D.O. (1985). Alexithymia and the split brain III, Global-level content analysis of fantasy and symbolization, *Psychotherapy-Psychosomatics, 44*, 89-94.

TenHouten, W.D., Hoppe, K.D., Bogen, J.E., & Walter, D.O. (1985). Alexithymia and the split brain IV, Gottschalk-Gleser content analysis, an overview, *Psychotherapy-Psychosomatics, 44*, 113-121.

TenHouten, W.D., Hoppe, K.D., Bogen, J.E., & Walter, D.O. (1986). Alexithymia: An experimental study of cerebral commissurotomy patients and normal control subjects, *American Journal of Psychiatry, 143*, 312-316.

Tucker, D.M., Watson, R.M., & Reilman, K.M. (1976). Affective discrimination and evocation in patients with right partial disease, *Neurology, 26*, 354.

Woolfolk, R.L., & Lehrer, P.M. (Eds.). (1984). *Principles and practices of stress management*, (pp. 227-245). New York, London: Guilford Press.

Zdenek, M. (1983). *The right brain experience*. New York: McGraw-Hill.

Frida Kahlo and Diego Rivera — The Transformation of Catastrophe to Creativity

Gladys Natchez

SUMMARY. Creativity is an elusive will of the wisp. We can neither summon it by will nor understand fully how it appears. Diego Rivera and Frida Kahlo, who became his wife, were two of the greatest artists in all of Mexico. In this paper I will compare in as much as I am able, the way in which the creativity of each one developed — through the influence of their history, their family, the way their personalities unfolded, and their reactions to their life experiences.

FRIDA'S EARLY YEARS

Frida was born on July 6, 1907, in a house on the corner of Londres and Allende streets in Coyoacan, Mexico. This house is now the Museo Frida Kahlo and remains faithful to the way she lived until she died at 47 years of age. Shortly after Frida was born her mother became ill and she was cared for by her older sisters, Matilde and Adriana. There was some discord in the family when Frida's father, Wilhelm, lost his lucrative commissions as a state architectural photographer. Besides financial problems, Senor Kahlo developed seizures, and his difficulties caused the family to suffer hard times.

When Frida was 6, she contracted polio. After she recovered, a doctor recommended physical exercise, and Wilhelm Kahlo, who had been unusually tender and concerned during his daughter's ill-

Gladys Natchez is Professor Emerita of the City College of the City University of New York and the author of several books on learning disability. She is in private practice in New York City, working with individuals, couples, and families. Mailing address: 263 West End Ave., New York, NY 10024.

ness, made sure that she took up sports including boxing and wrestling. Such activities were not respectable for young ladies in Mexico. Nevertheless her leg remained very thin. Although she wore little boots and four socks on the thinner calf, the children called her "peg leg." She responded with many curses, but Frida said that she became an "introverted creature" during that time.

When Frida was 31 she painted *Four Inhabitants of Mexico*, the walls of her family home. Frida sits on the dirt ground sucking her middle finger, clutching the folds of her skirt impassively. The four objects — a Judas figure, a pre-Colombian idol, a clay skeleton, and a straw horseman — are artifacts which signify the importance to her of her Mexican heritage. According to Frida's biographer, Hayden Herrera (1983), "They seem like a kind of family, offering comfort in a world that often felt void" (p. 18).

Of his six children, Frida was her father's favorite. He would encourage her intellectual adventurousness and liked her to accompany him on his photographic wanderings. She wrote,

> Many times when he went walking with his camera holding me by the hand, he would suddenly fall. I learned to help him during his attacks. On the one hand I would make sure that he breathed alcohol or ether and on the other I watched so his camera would not be stolen. He was an example to me of tenderness, dedication to work, and above all understanding of all my problems. (Herrera, p. 18)

Frida honored her father in 1952 with a *Portrait of Don Guillermo Kahlo*. The inscription reads:

> I painted my father Wilhelm Kahlo of Hungarian-German origin, artist-photographer by profession: in character generous, intelligent, and fine; valiant because he suffered for sixty years with epilepsy, but he never stopped working and he fought against Hitler with (persistence). His daughter Frida Kahlo.

In this picture, Frida has painted magnified cells which Herrera describes as "nuclei afloat in a swarm of small dark marks that suggest sperm." Herrera asks: "Did she merely want to refer to the fact that he was her biological progenitor? Or does the background suggest that Frida saw a connection between her father and primal energy?" (p. 21). In any case if they are only staccato marks they may simply suggest his inner unrest.

DIEGO'S EARLY LIFE

We will now examine Diego Rivera's early life to see what influences might be related to his prodigious artistic efforts. Diego's grandfather, father, and Diego himself all married women almost half their size and 10 to 30 years younger. Frida was 5 feet 3 inches, weighing 98 pounds, and was 22 years younger, while Diego was 6 feet plus, weighing 300 pounds or more.

Before Diego was born his mother had three miscarriages. They never expected her to come to term when she was pregnant with Diego. During labor his father prayed for a son to carry on his liberal ideas and to add to their income. Soon the news came — not only did Senor Rivera have a son — he had twin boys! The first born was named after his father, the other boy's name was Carlos.

Almost before Diego learned to walk and talk he began to draw. He climbed onto desks to find pencil and paper and scrawled over everything. His earliest memory was that he was drawing. As he grew taller, so many walls were defaced that his father gave him a room with unlimited chalk, and blackboards as high as he could reach. These were Diego's first murals. He also enjoyed arguing with parental commands and telling tall tales. This caused his pious mother and aunts to lament, but his father to admire.

When Carlos was two years old he took sick and died. His mother was so distraught she would not leave his grave. They had to rent a room at the cemetery for her. Because of his mother's grief, Diego was sent to live in the wilderness with an Indian nurse, Antonio (Rivera, 1960, p. 20). She was a wise woman who cherished him. She built up his health as well as his confidence. In his autobiography Diego says that all his life he loved her more than his own mother.

At the age of four, despite Diego's protests, his parents insisted he return home to Guanajuato. Diego seemed to get over this trauma and soon became the "wonder child" of his village. Guanajuato's inhabitants were stunned by his Jacobinism and his atheism. When his Great-Aunt Vicenta tried to eradicate such ideas and initiate him into church holiness by showing him the statues of the saints, he quipped, "Don't you see that this lady . . . is made of wood, Totota? How can (she) hear . . . ? She doesn't even have holes in her ears" (Wolfe, 1963, p. 19). His aunt fled in shame, but it is said that after she left he climbed on the steps of the altar and delivered an atheist harangue to the astonished crowd. When his father heard of this, Diego was admitted into his father's circle of Jacobin friends and would listen intently to their discussions. He was proud to answer questions concerning his views and listened closely, to the abstruse thoughts and long words that circled around him. Until Diego was eight, something close to 60 was the average age of his closest associates.

Diego's father was proud of his son and loved his inventiveness and scientific endeavors. An incident is told about the time his mother was again pregnant. His aunt wanted him out of the house because Senora Rivera was in labor, so she told him that he was going to have a brother that day and should go to the station to meet him. Diego waited for hours until he got disgusted. He asked the station master, who was a family friend, why his brother hadn't come. The station master said, "Ay . . . I forgot to tell you; your little sister has come. We sent her home . . . in a beautiful little box" (Wolfe, 1963, p. 21). Diego was mystified that he had seen no box and no little boy. When he reached home and saw the infant he said, "How ugly! Where is the box?" Anxious aunts ransacked the house, all they could find was an old shoe box. Diego became thoughtful: "You have told . . . lies. Now I know my sister did not come in a train or in a box. They gave mother an egg, and she warmed it in bed." When everyone laughed uproariously he became furious and wouldn't leave his room even to eat. A few days later his mother caught him trying to cut open the belly of a living mouse with a kitchen knife, "to find out," he explained, "where little mice come from and how they are made." The shock was too much for his mother, she was convinced that she had brought a monster into the world. His father on the other hand simply asked whether Diego's desire to understand birth had been so strong as to forget the pain caused to the mouse. Senor Kahlo then supplied sex and birth information to Diego. He immediately spent hours using this new information in drawing. Even this early in life he would draw nothing he did not understand.

Soon the family moved to Mexico City because of diminished opportunities in Guanajuato. Diego was inconsolable because there were no animals or trains to draw. He immediately developed scarlet fever and then typhoid. For a year he stopped drawing altogether. This pattern was to be repeated throughout his life. Whenever there was an interference with his painting he was likely to get sick. Even if he had no illness he became hypochondriacal and stopped work.

During his illness Diego was drawn to his devout Great-Aunt Vicenta. She took care of him and again urged him to go to church with her. She was joyous when he no longer objected. Actually, what caused him to be lost in contemplation was not the church service, but the beautiful votive offerings people painted to give thanks for some saintly intervention. He always loved his aunt, but he never became religious.

After Diego recovered, his mother insisted he attend a Catholic school. He received very high marks, but Padre Enrique was distraught upon hearing Diego's question about the Immaculate Conception. Diego had demanded, "How did the child Jesus leave her body, (since she was still) a virgin?" (p. 27). The good Father rushed to Diego's mother, telling her to give him religious training at home where he could not disturb the faith of less tough-textured minds. This convinced his mother and aunts that he was a devil. He was sent preemptively to the regular grammar school.

After two years, Diego knew that the only thing that he wanted was to study art. The boy was obviously determined — and his parents acquiesced with one stipulation: he would have to continue at the regular school and go to San Carlos Academy of Fine Arts at night. In addition to attending the two schools he sketched profusely after hours, "yet he completed elementary school with honors and won second prize in drawing" (p. 30).

SEEDS OF CREATIVITY

From Diego and Frida's early histories we can see hints of their transformation toward creative prowess. We know that before Diego was born Senora Rivera yearned for a live baby and her husband prayed for a son to carry on his life. We assume then, that Diego must have been especially welcomed into the world. When Diego's twin died and Senora Rivera went into the severe depression we know about, Diego developed rickets and lost weight. The abandonment by his mother and his brother, and later by his beloved nurse, must have taken its emotional and physical toll.

When Diego began the prolific drawing that has been mentioned, did he use this wealth of painting to smooth over the serious disruptions in his life? Did the abandonment by one person after another leave him in terror of separation? Was he so angry at leaving Antonia that he claimed throughout his life that he always loved her

more than his own mother? (Herrera, 1983, pp. 14-15). In his autobiography Diego never mentions the upset these events must have
caused him.

Frida had certain early experiences, similar to Diego's. When her
mother became ill after she was born, Frida was suckled by a Mexican Indian nurse. In later years she painted her as the mythic em-
bodiment of her Mexican heritage and remained attached to Mexican culture and folk ways. We know that when Frida contracted
polio she was isolated and lonely. She wrote in her diary at the time:

> I breathed vapor on (a window pane) . . . and with my finger
> . . . drew a "door" . . . I went . . . through (it and crossed)
> the . . . plain . . . until I . . . arrived at the dairy called "Pin-
> zon" . . . I entered by the "O" in Pinzon and went . . . into
> the interior of the earth where "my imaginary friend" was
> . . . waiting for me . . . I told her (all) my secrets . . . When I
> returned . . . I was happy . . . (I have) so vivid a memory of
> the little girl . . . (that even after 34 years I remember her
> clearly. (Herrera, 1983, p. 32)

Frida certainly transformed loneliness into a feeling of comfort
and companionship. Does her diary indicate that the dairy stood for
the breast's nourishing milk? Does the entering of the "O" in Pin-
zon and the "interior of the earth" represent her wish for her mother's womb? In any case Frida used her fertile imagination to con-
quer her barren situation and was able to convert despair into
pleasure, just as she did when her classmates teased her about her
infirmity.

We can see how both Frida and Diego fought hard for their own
unique paths even at this early period. Their strength may have
stemmed primarily from their loving fathers who gave them support, understanding, and wise guidance; and fought for them in op-
position to their spouses. This may partially account for Frida's and
Diego's enormous will, steadfast purpose, and unconventionality.
It may also be that since both Frida's and Diego's mothers did not
champion or approve them, their longing for maternal recognition
prompted Diego to paint and Frida to rebel.

FRIDA AND DIEGO – THE TEENAGE YEARS

At 15 Frida entered The National Preparatory School. Females
had just recently been admitted and Frida was one of 35 in a student

body of some 2000. Probably her mother resisted sending her to such an unprotected place, but Wilhelm Kahlo had no reservations. Having no son to fulfill his own disappointed ambitions, he pinned his hopes on Frida. Whether or not she understood this, Frida did indeed select a course that would lead to medical school.

It just so happened that Diego, then 36, was painting his mural in the Preparatoria's auditorium at the time. Fifteen-year-old Frida was fascinated by him and although the amphitheater where he painted was off limits, she managed to slip in. She taunted him by calling him "Old Fatso," but privately she predicted: "You'll see; now you don't pay attention to me, but one day I'll have a child by you" (Herrera, 1983, pp. 48-49).

As the years passed Frida worked, studied, played, and loved; yet she earned top grades. At 18 she grew more determined and her personality vibrated with fierce originality. In the same year, however, she suffered a cruel accident that affected her entire life.

Her sweetheart Alejandro Govez Arias, describes the horrible accident as follows:

> The electric train with two cars . . . hit (our) bus . . . It burst into a thousand pieces . . . Frida was thrown out. Something strange happened. (She) was totally nude. The collision had unfastened her clothes . . . I picked her up . . . and then I noticed with horror that Frida had a piece of iron in her body (from the broken handrail of the trolley.) A man said, "We have to take it out!" When he (removed it) Frida screamed so loudly that when the ambulance . . . arrived, her screaming was louder than the siren . . . Frida's condition was so grave that the doctors did not think they could save her. Her spinal column was broken in three places . . . Her right leg had eleven fractures and her right foot was crushed. The steel rail . . . literally skewered her body at the level of the abdomen, entering on the left side, it had come out through the vagina, "I lost my virginity" she said. (Herrera, 1983, p. 50)

In the hospital Frida told Alejandro: "Death dances around my bed at night. One must put up with it. I am beginning to grow accustomed to suffering." From the day of the accident, pain and fortitude became central themes in her life.

While Frida was in the hospital she wrote to Alejandro begging him to see her. He was angry because his friends told him Frida had an affair with another boy while she was going out with him. After months of quarreling Frida painted her first *Self Portrait* as a kind of love offering to him. She was 19 at the time. After that, they remained only friends.

From her 18th year on, Frida's life was grueling battle against deterioration. A friend who knew the medical records said that during Frida's life she had at least 32 operations and wore 27 casts at various intervals. Frida now had to lie flat on her back. "Since I was (so) young," she said, "this misfortune did not take on the character of a tragedy; I felt I had energies enough to do (something besides) studying to be a doctor. And so I began to paint" (p. 63). Her mother had a carpenter make an easel that could be attached to her bed since the plaster cast did not allow her to sit up. This was the beginning of Frida's biographical paintings. She was to illustrate her suffering, and her experiences throughout her life. According to her biographer's statement, "The girl whose ambition was to study medicine turned to painting as a form of psychological surgery" (p. 74).

* * *

When we looked at Diego in his teens, Frida was not yet born! We remember that he too decided to be an artist early in life. When Diego went to the Art Academy he improved his craft but after a while he became restless. When political riots began at the university, he saw an opportunity to leave school and as soon as the demonstrations ceased, Diego decided he was sick of formal study and quit school for good. He was 16 at the time. For four years he sketched the lush countryside of Mexico. He made one portrait of his mother but when she saw it she cried and claimed that not only was it ugly but her son couldn't possibly love her if he thought she looked like that. Despite this discouragement, Diego proceeded to paint everything that caught his eye. However, he himself was disappointed in his own work. He renounced oils and pastels; he experimented with other forms, but they all tortured him. He became discouraged and, as was his pattern, became ill. He even thought he was going blind. Hypochondria struck as usual in the wake of his painting inhibition. Did his mother's disapproval of his paintings reinforce this pattern?

Diego kept chafing at the bit. He wanted to go to Europe where he thought there were more accomplished painters but how could he get there without money? Toward the end of his wanderings he came into a piece of great luck that reads like a fairy tale. His father was now an inspector in the National Department of Public Health. His father's work happened to take him to the Governor of Vera Cruz whom Senor Rivera knew was a lover of the arts, so he told Diego to bring along some of his paintings.

The Governor was very impressed when he saw Diego's work and said, proudly, "We Veracruzanos know how to appreciate art and the (honor) it reflects on our fatherland. From today on, young man, you will receive a pension for European study" (Wolfe, 1963, pp. 40-41).

Diego rejoiced. He immediately sold all his paintings and lo! there was enough to buy his European passage. He was now 21 and with a light heart he set out for Spain. Diego wrote enthusiastic letters home, and sent newspaper clippings that praised his work. He also sent pictures to Governor Dehesa and through this Governor, Diego's reputation began to spread in Vera Cruz and in Mexico City.

Several months after Diego arrived in Spain, his mother wrote that she was coming to keep house for him. Diego was aghast. He wrote to his father saying that he had no time to spend with his mother, adding that he would be "eight months before I can stop working so hard." His mother answered: "Your father, his mother and your aunt reciprocate your affection and so does your unhappy mother, whom you will never have the displeasure to see again" (p. 47).

Six months later the Spanish painter Chicharro wrote a glowing report about Diego's work. Even though he sent this report to his mother with the note: "Receive these words as first fruits until I can send you something better, (because) I am trying to honor my father and mother . . . " (p. 48). I doubt that his mother was ever mollified.

Diego still agonized over finding the center of himself as an artist. Once a painting was completed, he berated himself and often beat his head against the walls of his studio. According to his biographer, Bertram Wolfe,

Diego became sick with . . . overwork. A glandular trouble, which probably explains his bulging eyes, was reinforced by anxiety and hypochondria. He was plagued by a succession of disorders, part real, part imaginary. Finally he became so disgusted he decided to leave Spain and take a long tour abroad.

FRIDA AND DIEGO – BEYOND THE TEENS

Now let us look at Frida and Diego beyond their troubled teens. After two years of convalescing, Frida was now 20. She could not continue her studies because her body was still bothersome and so she decided to try to paint for a living. At this time Frida happened to meet Diego at a gathering of some friends. He was now 42. She was pleased to see him again. He was telling his friends that he had traveled through Europe for 13 years trying to find his own milieu. He said he could not became a painter in the European style and after a long struggle he decided that he longed to paint the masses on Mexican Walls, particularly the Aztec culture and revolutionary scenes. He did indeed succeed in painting many political murals such as, *Before the Conquest* and *Mexico after the Conquest* to name only part of two walls. Diego depicts the figures in pre-conquest as rhythmical and flowing, while in post-conquest he interprets the stiffness, stress, and grimness of people's lives at that time.

Shortly after the meeting with Diego, Frida went to the building where he was working and called loudly for him to come down from the scaffold. Diego was impressed by her commanding voice and the way she looked, so he lumbered down. Without more ado she said:

> Look, I have not come to flirt or anything even if you *are* a woman chaser. I have come to show you my painting. If you are interested, . . . tell me . . . if not . . . I will go to work at something else. (Wolfe, 1963, p. 88)

After studying the paintings Diego told her she had talent. She replied that she had more paintings at home and asked him to come the next Sunday to visit. He agreed. Soon after that he began courting her and after a while they became engaged. Frida's mother could not accept her attachment to an ugly, fat, 42-year-old Communist nonbeliever – even a rich one. But Frida's father acquiesced because he liked Diego. Besides, Senor Kahlo was in financial difficulty and he knew that he would have trouble paying for Frida's continued medical expenses.

Diego belonged to the Communist Party at the time but he also wanted to accept a government commission. So he decided not only to quit the party but to preside over his own expulsion. Dromundo describes the scene:

> I, Diego Rivera, general secretary of the Mexican Communist
> Party, accuse the painter Diego Rivera of collaborating with
> the petit-bourgeois government of Mexico and of having ac-
> cepted a commission to paint the stairway of the National Pal-
> ace of Mexico. This contradicts the politics of the Comintern
> and therefore the painter Diego Rivera should be expelled.
> (Herrera, 1983, p. 102)

However, Diego always remained a Communist in spirit.

Frida did not paint much in the early years of her marriage. Diego took all of her time nursing him when he fell ill or despondent, being at his side and appraising his work (incidentally, he had the utmost confidence in her opinions). Thus she submerged herself in a strong symbiotic stance.

Frida now longed for a baby and became pregnant in the first year of their marriage. Unfortunately she had to have an abortion because the fetus was in the wrong position. Another troubling aspect for Frida was that she suspected Diego of having an affair with his young assistant. She realized that the misfortunes that marred her childhood would be equaled or surpassed by miseries in her adult life. In her own words she stated: "I suffered two grave accidents in my life, one in which a streetcar knocked me down . . . The other accident is Diego" (Herrera, 1983, p. 107).

According to Frida's biographer, Frida despaired at her husband's infidelities, but there is no question that even when she hated him, Frida adored him. This did not mean eclipsing herself because Rivera admired strong and independent women; he expected Frida to have her own ideas, her own friends, her own activities, but at the same time to take care of him completely. Quite a task! That she tried to earn her living and kept her maiden name pleased him. And if "he did not open car doors for her, he (*did* open) worlds."

When Frida got married she favored the Tehuana costume as a new self-image *Self Portrait*. It pleased Diego and besides, the long skirts were a hiding place for her deformed leg. Frida's elaborate dress signified her compensation for her body's deficiencies, for her feelings of fragmentation, and at the same time it was "an affirmation of her love of life and a signal of her . . . defiance of death."

Diego was becoming well-known during this time, particularly in America. He received a commission to paint for the San Francisco Stock Exchange Luncheon Club, where he depicts the agriculturist Luther Burbank, the ranchers, miners, mechanics, and gold prospectors as well as oil wells and steamships. An opulent woman represents California; one of her hands opens the subsoil to the miner and the other offers fruits of the earth. A worker-student holds a model airplane probably suggesting the future. Diego painted another mural for the San Francisco Art Institute. The most interesting part of this last fresco is the rear view of Diego sitting on the scaffold. Bertram Wolfe (1963) comments, "How a man must know himself to be able to render his back so faithfully" (p. 291). (The painting is divided to show the architectural construction. In the center of the base are an engineer, an architect, and the donor; the sides depict raw material and workers. Above, draftsmen and metal workers raise the steel skeleton and above sculptors give form to the stone; in the center of the scaffold painters and masons create the gigantic figure of a worker. He grasps the machine with one hand and a lever with the other.)

Diego received other United States commissions. Henry Ford asked for a mural at the Detroit Institute of Arts and John D. Rockefeller invited him to paint at the RCA building. As Max Kozloff put it: "Nowhere else has avowedly proletarian art been so loftily sponsored by capitalist patronage" (Herrera, 1983, p. 115).

While Diego was painting in Detroit, Frida had another miscarriage and was told never again to become pregnant. The experience reinforced her hatred for "Gringolandia," as she called the United States. She hated the culture, the pace, the terrible waste, and the noise. She begged and begged Diego to return to Mexico but he refused. To overcome his rejection Frida produced the painting, *Henry Ford Hospital* (1932). Frida lies naked on the bed, lying on a bloody sheet. Attached to six vein-like strands are a fetus, a pink torso which Frida says is "my idea of explaining the insides of a woman," two spinal columns which refer to her injured backbone, and a snail which Frida explains is the "slowness of the miscarriage." The orchid was drawn, she said, because Diego gave her one in the hospital and it signified to her both sexuality and sentimentality.

After four years when all Diego's work was accomplished in America, Frida urged him once more to go back home. He said absolutely not; he had fallen in love with industrial America. He claimed that he had never been happier and that he would stay in the United States indefinitely. But after badgering him and badgering him, Frida finally wore him down and he grudgingly returned home.

Several months after their return, Diego engaged in another affair. Frida had a sister Cristina whom she loved dearly. She considered Cristina her best friend and supporter. And it was Cristina whom Diego chose to model for him and with whom he had an extended liaison. Frida was devastated. She couldn't believe that the two people she loved most in the world would betray her. In hurt and despair she depicted her pain and anguish in the painting, *A Few Small Nips*. The picture was painted after Frida read a news account of a murderer who threw his girlfriend on a cot and stabbed her 24 times. When he was interrogated by the police, he said: "But it was only a few small nips." Splotches of blood are all over the painting continuing onto the frame. Frida said that she represented the murderer as a macho and the victim as chingada. Chingada is a curse word meaning "the screwed one." She said she felt sympathy with the murdered woman since she herself had been "murdered by life" (Herrera, 1983, p. 115).

In fury and vengeance, Frida cut off her beautiful hair and renounced her Tehuana dress. She assumed a man's clothing (*Cropped Hair*). The suit is so big on her that it probably belonged to Diego. By destroying the attributes of female sexuality, Frida tries to diminish it. She holds the scissors near her genitals, perhaps to excise the most important part of herself that is capable of loving.

Diego and Frida both became sick in this period, probably over the affair. Actually Diego had engaged in the same betrayal long before he knew Frida when he took as mistress the younger sister of his then common-law wife, Lupe. It hardly seems accidental that such an act occurs twice. (I am indebted to Dr. Alma Bond [personal communication] for the suggestion that Diego and his *own* younger sister may have had incestuous relations at one time and this may have been a repetition of the pattern.) In connection with this phenomenon, Diego wrote in his autobiography, "If I loved a woman, the more I loved her, the more I wanted to hurt her. Frida was only the most obvious victim of this disgusting trait" (Herrera, 1983, p. 183).

To understand Diego's statement, it is necessary to explore Rivera's sado-masochistic character. He enjoyed women but cut off his loving feelings for fear of engulfment. The fear was stronger and more available than his love (Bond, 1984, p. 47). As usual, this probably originated from his relationship with his mother. The closer he became to Frida the more fearful he was that he would lose himself. Also, Diego could never tolerate giving up autonomy.

Submitting to Frida's urging to return to Mexico must have touched off wild unconscious anxiety. Perhaps he then ran to Cristina for compensation. It is fascinating to observe that since he used the same pattern with both his wives, he accomplished two triumphs. In both instances he could have his wife's loving representative and yet need not fear the loss of his identity.

On the other hand Frida was a perfect foil in this situation. Like every good masochist, she acknowledged her loving feelings for Diego, but was unaware of repressing any fear of losing her identity. She could submerge herself in the service of love and remain ignorant of cheating her own needs and wishes. Does it sound as though they both needed a good analyst in the house?

During this period, Frida and Diego's meetings were awkward. She did her best to forget but she couldn't. Several years later she completed a picture called *Memory* (1937). In it a sword is piercing her heart. On one side she shows the Tehuana dress that she does not wear for Diego; on the other side hangs her schoolgirl uniform. Frida has no hands, which may symbolize her helplessness. On the ends of the sword sit two cupids showing how hard love is, while on the floor lies a huge broken heart which has been torn from her chest, leaving a gaping hole. Blood flows to the mountains beyond and to the sea in front.

Frida began to paint prodigiously at this point, and Diego said, "During the two years we lived apart, Frida turned out some of her best work, sublimating her anguish in her painting" (Herrera, 1983, p. 277).

Diego was now in California where he had to flee because he was accused of radical activity. Frida's ill health haunted him and he spoke to a Dr. Eloesser, who had become a friend and medical advisor when Frida and Diego first visited in California. After hearing what Diego told him, the Doctor wrote the following letter to Frida:

> Diego loves you very much and you love him. It is also the case, and you know it better than I, that besides you, he has two great loves — one, painting — two, women in general. He has never been nor will he ever be, monogamous . . . Reflect Frida. If you think that you could accept the facts the way they are, could live with him under these conditions . . . could submerge your jealousy in work . . . (then marry him.) (Herrera, 1983, p. 298)

The Doctor also urged her to come to San Francisco where he might be able to treat her. Frida took the doctor's advice and went to San Francisco where Diego welcomed her. Despite their ups and downs they made a valiant effort to reconcile. Finally, Frida told a friend, "He wants me to (remarry) because he says he loves me more than any other girl so I decided to marry him" (p. 299). She stipulated, however, that she wanted no more sex with him because "all the images of his other women (would flash through her mind)."

FRIDA AND DIEGO — LATER DEVELOPMENTS OF CREATIVITY

Although Frida cursed and bemoaned her fate in endless harangues, she used her vigor to transform her anguish and fury into painting. How dramatic that from the time she was a young girl with a tragic handicap she absorbed the full meaning of her plight, yet summoned sufficient energy to welcome love, life, work, and play.

From whence did all this come? We know how much Frida strongly identified with her father and it must have led her not only to paint but to look for strong, revered men all her life. Besides Trotsky, she was intimate with the prominent photographer Nicholas Murray, Noguchi, and others.

As for Frida's mother, we know that Frida never had a kinship with her. Note that as far as I can determine, Frida never painted her own mother and there is little written about their relationship. Perhaps Frida's mother loved her, but my guess is that Senora Kahlo never believed Frida would do anything to make her mother proud. This may have engendered guilt in Senora Kahlo. More than that, Frida's mother, who disapproved so much of Frida's unconventionality, may have been relieved and even hopeful, albeit unconsciously, that the serious injuries her daughter suffered would impede this rebellious quality.

Besides having little rapport with her mother, Frida was frustrated by not being able to have a baby. No matter how she tried, she never had the "Little Diego" she yearned for. She sublimated this yearning by becoming a mother to her husband and treating him like a child, catering to his every whim, making him special meals, and even bathing him. In *The Love Embrace* Frida finally possesses Diego in the way that presumably worked best for them. In the painting Diego is a big baby lying contentedly in her maternal lap.

She writes, "I am the embryo . . . that . . . engendered him. . . . At every moment he is my child" (Herrera, 1983, p. 375). Painting took second place to taking care of him. In this picture Frida is embraced by the large pre-Colombian idol, perhaps because she felt in need of nurturing too, while the medallion in Diego's forehead is Frida's idea of his unusual "informing eye."

After her divorce Frida slowly began disengaging from Diego. To a close friend she said she had now begun to paint in earnest and "my paintings are the (frankest) expression of myself. I have painted without desire for glory or ambition . . . " (p. 317). Perhaps Frida did not seek glory, but it seems to me she longed to be recognized as an important person. If her mother wouldn't recognize her, perhaps through her painting others would.

The painting, *Remembrance of an Open Wound* suggests that Frida transformed herself further from a child to a woman. She is no longer the passive female; instead she seems to flaunt her wounds as she stares out at the viewer.

It is interesting that while most of her work reflects sorrow and tragedy, in her last years, she turned to what she named *Naturaliza Viva*, "alive lifes" or "alive still lives." These "lifes" seem to show a more serene sense than her earlier pictures.

Now let us look at Diego's development. In Jung's (1954) words, "Diego never faltered from the fidelity of his own being" (p. 173). How did this happen? First of all, we remember that from the time he was a toddler he would not accept explanations that did not make sense to him. Second, he refused to obey commands that he felt were unreasonable whether from parents, relatives, teachers, or other authorities. We recall, too, his early traumas of loss with his own mother, brother, and nurse. His treatment of women seemed to stem directly from these wounds. He came to disdain them, probably so he could overcome his deep hurt, and then he came to dread their loss. As a result, he always had nurturing women around him (he had four wives, two of whom were common-law spouses for a time — and countless mistresses.) Interestingly enough, he often related to them more maternally than sexually claiming that "sex is like urinating; I don't know why everyone makes such a fuss about it." He claimed that he could not help his constant infidelities which he knew would hurt the women he loved. This may have been related to his voracious appetite both literally with food and psychologically with gathering crowds around him. He must have also covered over his feelings of anxiety by devoting himself to his work, which consumed on the average 14-18 hours a day.

Diego had no tragedy befall him the way Frida did. All his anguish was in the service of becoming the man he wanted to be. He finally found his inner meaning by painting revolutionary themes for human betterment. This must have been his way of identifying with his father's radical philosophy and avowing his deep love and admiration for him.

We can see Frida and Diego's thrust toward growth in creating their own lives. They overcame their difficulties sometimes by repression, sometimes by devotion to work, sometimes by accepting their assets and limitations, and yet forcing themselves to go on. No doubt some of this energy stemmed from the universal wish for immortality. They took risks; they followed their deeper feelings — in short, they became as free and creative as they knew how.

THE RIVERAS' LAST YEARS

In their last years, the Riveras settled into a reasonably happy pattern, no longer determined mainly by Diego. Having gained in confidence and independence, Frida became more maternal than wifely. Diego at this point was busy with his commissions and his women. There was no doubt that Frida meant more to him than any other woman and he knew she was his mainstay, but he had to have many others to cater to his boundless needs.

Frida now turned more to women lovers than to men. Perhaps this relates to her deep longing for a mother. Also her physical state may have made it difficult to have penetration with a man at this stage. According to Tibol, she consoled herself by cultivating the friendships of (the very) women with whom Diego had enormous relations: Guadalupe, Cristina, Dorothy Hale, Dolores del Rio, and others.

Each year Frida had more health problems. A Mexican doctor placed her in a steel apparatus. It was one of the 27 corsets Frida wore during her life. The steel corset is depicted in *The Broken Column*: "The nails driven into her body portray her utter anguish. . . . In the bloody gap of her body is a broken Ionic column suggesting her deformed spine."

With all this ghastliness, Frida also had to endure an amputation of her leg six months later. As usual, she lifted some of her despair by ordering luxurious red leather boots with Chinese gold embroidered trim and little bells on the cuffs. She not only learned to walk, but soon twirled around in them. Her nurse commented that she had never seen anyone overcome disaster the way Frida did. Regaled in her boots, she forced herself to paint for four to five hours a day even though she was often confined to a wheelchair.

Lola Alvarez Bravo, who owned the Galeria Arte Contemporaneo, realized that Frida's death was near and wished to honor her while she was alive. Frida was enthusiastic when she heard, and her health actually improved for a few days.

When the night of the opening drew near, Frida was so weak that her doctors forbade her to go out. Frida paid no attention and sent her huge four-poster bed ahead to the gallery. Since the bed itself was a work of art that Frida had always continued decorating, Lola Bravo rearranged all the paintings and the bed became part of the show.

At the opening Frida was carried into her exhibition on a stretcher and placed on her bed in style. She was in her glory and held court in all her magnificence. Diego said of it,

> For me, (it was) the most thrilling event of 1953. . . . Even I was impressed when I saw all her work together. . . . (But) I thought afterwards that she must have realized she was bidding good-bye to life. (Herrera, 1983, p. 410)

Frida finally faced the fact that her death was imminent. In the final entry of her diary Frida drew a black angel rising to the sky with the words, "I hope the exit is joyful—and I hope never to come back, Frida." (p. 431).

A week after her 47th birthday, Frida Kahlo was dead. Diego sat beside her all night and was with her to the end. According to his biographer, "He became an old man in a few hours, pale and ugly" (p. 433). For once he refused to talk to reporters, turning his face to the wall and remaining silent.

Frida's friends dressed her in a black Tehuana costume. They braided her hair with ribbons and flowers; they adorned her with jewels.

Andreas Iduarte, her old schoolmate from the Preparatoria, was then the director of the National Institute of Fine Arts and gave special permission to Diego to honor Frida by having her lie in state at this magnificent building. He made one condition, however: Rivera must promise that there would be no political demonstrations. Diego assented. However he did not keep his word. Iduarte found the casket covered with a shiny red flag bearing the hammer and sickle in the middle of a white star and the crowd was singing the International. A hullabaloo ensued and in the end Iduarte lost his directorship as a result of the incident. Instead of remorse, Diego was delighted because the act gained him readmittance to the Communist Party. As we can see, Diego rarely was ambivalent and when he wanted something he cared not about the consequences.

Diego carried out Frida's wish to be cremated and as the time approached, Monroy recalls, "When the door of the oven opened to receive the cart with Frida in it, there was an infernal heat that forced us all to press up against the back wall. But Diego did not move." It was at this point that the most grotesque scene occurred. A friend recalls, "Everyone was hanging on to Frida's hands. They threw themselves on top of her and yanked at her fingers in order to take off her rings because they wanted to have something that belonged to her." Cristina became hysterical. Then she began to scream and shriek more wildly because when her sister's body slid toward the oven, the intense heat made her sit up and her glazing hair stood out from her face in an aureole. Diego sketched Frida's silvery skeleton before her ashes dispersed. In his autobiography he wrote: "July 13, 1954, was the most tragic day of my life. I had lost my beloved Frida, forever. . . . Too late, now, I realized that the most wonderful part of my life had been my love for Frida" (Rivera, 1960, p. 285).

After Frida died Diego mourned for a time but then recovered somewhat. He had for many years been close to one Emma Hurtado who owned the gallery that sold his paintings. After one year had passed, when he was 69, Diego married Emma, this time secretly, with no fanfare.

His energy was waning and in 1956 he decided to go to Russia. When he arrived he was proud to be readmitted as a Communist again. Ironically, it was here in Moscow that Diego thought of reconciling with the Church over a mural he had painted years ago in Mexico at the Hotel del Prado with a sign saying: "God does not Exist." It caused such a furor that the fresco was covered with a screen for years. When Diego returned to Mexico he made arrangements to erase the motto. It was astonishing. He avowed in Moscow that he was a Communist. Then when he was asked in Mexico why he decided to erase the motto he stated, "I am a Catholic." He placated Rome and Moscow in one fell swoop.

In September 1957, Diego suffered a blood clot that paralyzed his right arm. On the 24th of November, he called Emma to his side. "Should I raise the bed?" she asked. He answered, "On the contrary, lower it." These were his last words.

When the populace received word of Diego's death, crowds thronged the rotunda of the Palace of Fine Arts where he was ensconced. Both the Communist Party and the Mexican Government contributed their respective remarks at the cremation ceremony.

Diego's and Frida's works will live on forever with a vitality of their own. And so we leave Diego with his flaws and his greatness; Frida with her sorrows and her bravery—and know we can go to their paintings whenever we wish to recapture the breadth and grandeur of their vision.

SUMMARY

In this paper we have traced the lives of Frida Kahlo and Diego Rivera to examine some of the factors that led to their particular creativity and to some of the factors that promote creativity in general.

The first factor is the mutual admiration of Frida and Diego for their fathers. Frida's veneration influenced her to idolize and submit to revered and distinguished men and to follow in an aspect of her father's profession, namely painting. (He was an artist-photographer as she called him.) Diego basked in his father's liberal attitude, support, understanding, and generosity. He learned independence of thought and fearlessness of action through his father's example.

Another factor in Frida's and Diego's creativity suggests that their fathers' loving concern and wisdom must have counteracted their mothers' restrictions and narrowness. Both mothers were rigid and disapproving of their children whereas the fathers were deeply involved and encouraging. Thirdly, the enormous energy that both artists enjoyed was in all likelihood genetic. Their energy was irrepressible: it allowed Diego to work 17-18 hours a day nonstop; it allowed Frida to paint whether in a cast, a hospital bed, or a wheelchair. Fourthly, both artists allowed their true feelings and actions to emerge even when such things were forbidden by authorities, family, society, or convention. This encouraged them to tread their unique paths relentlessly, with minimum restraint. According to Jung (1954) this soleness of purpose is the ultimate in living a creative life and ultimately becoming one's true self. Diego's will was resolute, decisive, and overwhelming from infancy. He brooked no interference; he defied consequences. Frida's will allowed her to overcome severe illness from a tragic accident that crippled her.

Frida started out as a frisky, happy youngster. When she contracted polio it brought out her contemplative and imaginative side. Later her accident turned her into a determined, strong character who strove to overcome the injuries to her spine and leg. Before her accident she had wanted to be a doctor. When her health precluded this she thought of painting. She knew Diego slightly and went to him for advice as to her possible talent. Diego encouraged her and finally they fell in love and married. Frida did not paint much after her marriage. Instead she lived in Diego's shadow for many years. When she discovered his infidelities she could not bear living with him and they divorced.

Gradually Frida found her inner self as she started living independently. Both Diego and Frida were devastated at living apart, however, and after two years they remarried. Most of Frida's paintings reflect the sorrow and tragedy she experienced during their separation. Before her death she wrote:

> I (want) above all to transform (my painting) so . . . it will be something useful, since until now I have painted only the honest expression of my own self . . . I should struggle . . . in the direction of helping the Revolution. The only real reason to live. (Herrera, 1983)

She never fulfilled this transition, however. Instead she turned to what she called "*Naturaliza Viva*" — "alive lifes" or "alive still lifes." In *Fruits of the Earth,* her fruits are alive and sexual. In *Viva la Vida* which she painted in the last years of her life, Frida portrays luscious watermelon rounds with juicy centers. She does show one piece of the melon with jagged edges, which may or may not signify the jaggedness of her life. The "alive lifes" may mean that Frida came to some surcease within herself at last and perhaps was making peace with death.

In contrast, Diego never wavered from painting. He absolutely had to — nothing could stop him except the times when he despaired about his work. Then he would become ill or hypochondriacal. He finally found his milieu by depicting the suffering and history of the common human being.

I have tried to generalize about the creative process from Diego's and Frida's lives. Baldly stated, the creative experience is a way of fulfilling the longing for ongoing growth and new experiences. According to Rank (1975) the creative person (or anyone who is uninhibited enough) yearns for new ways in becoming fully himself or herself. This longing, this unending search, has both conscious and unconscious motivation related to the wish for immortality; it also derives its strength from the sexual drive as Freud has told us in many contexts. So powerful are these drives that one is constantly seeking to protect oneself against negative occurrences.

Lest this all sound too simple, let us remember that no productive life is accomplished without market upheaval. We realize that torment as well as excitement stem from the creative process itself, for such work is capable of engendering inferiority and terror unless it can be proven at least acceptable. But even then, guilt and shame can interfere. The creator risks having gone too far; perhaps one considers oneself too arrogant or too unconventional or whatever. Thus we can begin to see the anguish involved in creating and being responsible for fulfilling our lives. We know that if we do not follow our unique path we live in a death grip; if we take our life in our own hands we have the joy of creation and also the terror of not having done enough. Frida and Diego are examples of overcoming their stumbling blocks and making peace with what they could not do. Both artists trod their unique paths with minimum repression. They took risks; they followed their deepest feelings; and they did the work they wanted wherever possible; in short, they became as free and creative as they knew how.

REFERENCES

Bond, A. (1984). *Aspects of psychoanalysis*. Freeport, NY: Exposition Press.
Herrera, H. (1983). *Frida*. New York: Harper & Row.
Jung, C. (1954). *The development of personality*. New York: Bollingen Foundation.
Rank, O. (1975). *Art and artist*. New York: Agathon Press.
Rivera, D. (1960). *My art, my life*. New York: The Citadel Press.
Wolfe, B. (1963). *The fabulous life of Diego Rivera*. New York: Stein & Day.